Who Let This Disaster in My Classroom?

Who Let This Disaster in My Classroom?

*A Practical Guide for Online Instructors
and Some Funny Stories along the Way*

CASSANDRA J. SMITH

RESOURCE *Publications* · Eugene, Oregon

WHO LET THIS DISASTOR IN MY CLASSROOM?
A Practical Guide for Online Instructors and Some Funny Stories along the Way

Resource Publications
A Division of Wipf and Stock Publishers
199 W. 8th Ave., Suite 3
Eugene, OR 97401

www.wipfandstock.com

ISBN 13: 978-1-60608-577-6

Manufactured in the U.S.A.

Contents

Acknowledgments

I WANT TO THANK my Lord and Savior Jesus Christ. I had an epiphany when I was writing this book. Everything that happened in my life was for this moment. All my experiences and ideas come from my creator. I thank you, Father, because the glory you have given me returns back to you; I humbly thank you for my many gifts. I want to thank my husband, who has helped me in my writing career and spiritual growth and has given me the gift of laughter; it is priceless. It looks like we are popular for real, baby—you and me.

I thank my parents. My father is a man of few words. "You are looking very prosperous," and "You can do it," reverberated in my mind throughout the tough times. I love you, Dad. My mother, I want to thank you. You are the love of my life. I thank you, Mom, for showing me my true self. You went to bat for me even when you did not know why. You are my precious gem. My sisters and brother, I want to thank you for being interested in all my projects and saying, "That sounds great, Chickie," even if it did not. Bee, Jan, and Zaboy, you carried me. To all my family (grandmother, aunts, uncles, nieces, nephews, and cousins) and friends, you were there for me from the inception of this project. You saw my light. You are jewels.

I want to thank my publisher, Wipf and Stock, for saying yes. All it takes is one yes and someone to care. Finally, I want to thank my students. This book would not exist without you. You helped me grow as an instructor. No matter the challenges we might have had, please know that as soon as I saw your name on my class roster, I prayed for each one of you that you would pass my class successfully—and that you would do well in your careers. To my fellow online instructors, your heart has led you to this career. I pray that your faith will not fail in your students or yourself; you are not alone.

—Cassie

1

100-mph Winds

IT WAS ONE OF those days when I questioned everything about online learning. Teaching had been going relatively well for close to two years. Then I started teaching a psychology course, and that is when everything went awry. I wondered to myself, *Who let this disaster in my classroom?* I'm sure that when you read this title you will automatically think of students with major issues. Yes, there are these kinds of students out there. But it was everything about teaching online in general that started to disturb me. It disturbed me so much so that it made me pose questions to myself such as: *Am I being effective as an online instructor?* In some of the classes I taught, the curricula were basically designed for me. I am a technical writer by trade, with a background in journalism. Therefore, I was accustomed to writing my own scripts in whatever form (i.e., curricula, news scripts, training material, etc.). At first I eagerly welcomed the idea that I did not have to create my own curriculum, only teach it. But then that day arrived when I questioned everything about distance education. I questioned the quality of online content. I questioned students' retention of the curricula. I questioned my commitment to my chosen career. I questioned the sincerity of students' interaction with their peers. I questioned the level of faculty support from the school. I questioned myself as a teacher. After all the questions and no answers, I wanted to walk away from my love.

I decided to write this book to chronicle my journey as an online instructor. I also wanted to let you know that as an online instructor, you are not alone in cyberspace. It may seem lonely at times when you are teaching online, but your fellow online instructors are there sensing your joys and frustrations. The most important reason for writing this book was to offer suggestions to help you get through the tough times when teaching online. This book provides a candid look at real-life stories and issues that I have encountered as an online instructor. Although these are factual accounts, they do contain fictionalized characters and material to protect the individuals involved, as well as myself. I decided to be proactive and take charge of my distance-learning teaching experiences. After all, I was and still am an online instructor, and I absolutely love teaching.

WHY THE TERM DISASTER?

There is a certain disconnect in the online environment. Unlike a traditional setting, a student or an instructor cannot obtain a quick response when needed. For an instructor, this can be just as disturbing as it is for the student. There are many situations where online teaching can feel like a disaster—when there are students asking questions and it seems that you cannot respond expeditiously; if there are students asking the same questions and you cannot clarify them immediately; if there is a misunderstanding among students; if there is a misunderstanding with regard to assignments; if a student has pushed you below professionalism; if there is a need for clarification between you and your administrator; and if you have typed the same answer to a question several times—even after you have explained the same information in class. The term disaster relates to the possibilities of what can spiral out of control through correspondence. This book will explain how to create effective e-mails in your online classroom; how to reduce conflict in your online classroom; how to stay motivated in your online classroom—especially when you are exhausted; how to design effective discussion board questions; and in essence, how to create pedagogical practices that you can implement in your online class. I also write about some of my most challenging yet funny student disasters.

Throughout this book, I chose to use metaphoric disasters. We all have had events in our lives that might have been disasters. If we were lucky, lives were not lost but a transition occurred that caused us to learn. The same concept applies to teaching disasters. In the process of the disaster, we learn to renew our commitment to online learning, reconnect with our students, and revive our classrooms before, during, and after the disaster.

LOVE FOR E-LEARNING

I fell in love with distance education in 2002. A friend of mine had some material from the University of Phoenix. He was thinking about returning to school online to obtain his graduate degree. I asked him how it worked. As with most novice distance-education participants, I wondered how anyone could attend classes online. I was perplexed by how I could submit assignments, interact with students, contact my instructor, and submit quality work. How would it be designed? I had an abundance of questions, and to my surprise, I was very interested. My friend did not have my answers. He was going to read the information and let me know what he discovered. A couple of days passed, and I still found myself thinking about our conversation. I was anticipating the answers to my questions and wanted to know more about attending school online. I decided to research the information myself.

I was semi-interested in returning to school to obtain my graduate degree, but I was in need of something different, and this appeared to fit the description. I did not want to attend a traditional college as I had in undergraduate school. I eventually called the University of Phoenix. After speaking with an excited advisor, I was immediately enrolled. I asked about the programs, particularly the Master of Arts in education with a concentration in adult education. I am still not sure why I chose education; it simply resonated in my spirit. Teaching college was always my secondary career plan in the event that my primary career plan, writing or becoming an actress, did not come to fruition. I know this might seem a bit odd, but it is true. I always dreamed of being on stage or in film acting out a magnificent script, preferably one that I had written. I was becoming older and it wasn't happening, so I knew that it was time to implement my secondary plan. I always felt comfortable in the collegiate environment. While some of my friends and peers appeared to dread attending college for another four years after high school, I was eager to embark on this journey. For as long as I could remember, academia had always attracted me, as a student and as a potential instructor. I figured if I obtained a master's degree, then I could teach entry-level college students.

I enrolled in school, and thus began my journey. In class, I often heard the term distance education. Even though I was participating in this new age of learning, I was clueless as to what it involved. It eventually dawned on me—two classes into graduate school, during my instructional design class—that what I was engaging in daily was distance education at the University of Phoenix. I was sold right then and there on this type of learning! I love learning about designing online curricula, and I love interacting online. I had discovered both my loves in one setting: writing and teaching. At this point, I truly knew that I wanted to teach online as well as in a traditional classroom.

After receiving my degree after nearly two years of graduate school, I began my search for a full-time teaching job. There was a grace period at the University of Phoenix for alumni to teach, so I couldn't apply for any teaching positions there. This would have been ideal because I really enjoyed attending the college. Of course, teaching jobs were scarce. Most colleges wanted an instructor to have a terminal degree and a number of education credits in his/her undergraduate degree. My undergraduate degree is in communication. My graduate degree is in education. Had I obtained both degrees in education or communication, it would have made the transition into the job market smoother; I would have had enough credits to teach in one or the other discipline. At that point, it didn't matter what I taught; I just wanted to teach. Since that didn't work out, I started searching for online teaching jobs consistently. The only positions that I found online were part-time adjunct teaching jobs. I thought to myself, *Is this some type of cruel joke? If so, it is not funny. Why aren't there any full-time teaching jobs online? Hasn't anyone heard of distance education? Surely this type of learning is pervasive.* Keep in mind that I'd just heard of distance education.

I managed to find a college looking for part-time online instructors. I applied for the position and was surprised when I received an e-mail about a telephone interview. Today full-time online teaching jobs are more common, even though there aren't many, but when I was looking, there were few schools that would accept an instructor with only a master's degree, let alone offer a full-time online teaching position. I started teaching at one online college in April 2007 and eventually started teaching at another in October 2007. This began my wonderful, challenging, and mixed-emotion online instructor journey.

You will notice that I refer to meteorology terms throughout this book. This is because they describe my potential and oftentimes occurring disasters. I also use other types of disaster terms that could cause chaos, but somehow the weather disasters seem to describe some of my students and situations perfectly!

BEING AN ADJUNCT

Being a part-time instructor can be difficult when you have a full-time job. I worked full-time as a technical writer and additionally taught four classes at one point. The money was great, but I am sure that you can imagine that I was exhausted.

I worked 8:00 a.m. to 5:00 p.m. as a technical writer—writing online medical coding training material. I taught two English courses at one college and two academic communication courses at another college. To protect the privacy of the colleges, I will refer to them as college A and college B. At college A, as an online instructor, I had to respond to 25 percent of my students in the discussion board forums (or discussion board), which are essentially areas where students answer assigned questions in the school's distance education software. I had to interact in the discussions with my students to show that I was present as their instructor, pose questions, and keep the discussion board forum active. I had to grade students' discussion responses and grade all written assignments, if I was the writing specialist for my course, and I was on several occasions. It was extra income on top of the part-time teaching salary. Also, I had to post up-to-date announcements, answer questions, and compose a weekly lecture. Usually, I had a total of fifteen responses for the discussion questions each week and more to go beyond my student interaction requirements. Since I was teaching two courses, this totaled thirty responses for the discussion board forum at college A.

At college B, I had to make a minimum of five posts to the discussion responses each week, and that was great! Since I was teaching two classes, that was a total of ten posts. In this class, I had to grade students' discussion board forum responses and written assignments. Also, I had to host live sessions on a synchronous platform with students. Students had weekly scenarios to read, and then they attended the live chat sessions to discuss the scenarios. It was a way to interact with the students for an hour. This involved more preparation than any of the other tasks. I had to prepare questions to ask regarding the weekly scenarios and monitor the responses, as you will read about in the student disaster chapters.

I guess by now you are wondering how I maintained such a hectic schedule, interacted with my students, graded papers, and handled my disasters. What can I say? I am superwoman! Realistically, it was hard work. As I stated above, I have a passion for teaching online, so I made it work. Here's what I did to stay ahead and work smart.

- During lunch time, I checked my e-mails and responded to students who did not require detailed resolution. The e-mails that did require class research and problem solving I resolved after work.

- When I left my full-time job each day, I enjoyed time with my husband and ate dinner before attending class. I also took an hour for "me time" to pray and gather my thoughts and basically take a mental break.

- Usually, I was online by 8:00 p.m. I checked e-mails and interacted with students, but I did not attempt to complete all my required discussion responses in one evening. On the nights when I had the live sessions, I only checked and responded to e-mails that were sent directly to my inbox and that were in the discussion question forum in the class; I did not work on many discussion board responses.

- The weekends were my time for play and work. Usually, I spent the mornings doing class work, preparing for the live sessions, preparing weekly lectures, and interacting in the discussion boards. I found that students did not ask questions on the weekend as much as they did on the weekdays. I guess they were out enjoying the weekend or completing assignments for the upcoming week. Sunday evening was weekly class preparation and assignment grading time as well. I had a schedule mapped out for teaching online.

Basically, this is how I constructed and maintained my teaching schedule. It was hard work, but I was committed to teaching online. Also, I enjoyed teaching at the different colleges; it made my routine less monotonous.

2

Preparation for the Storm

IF YOU KNOW THAT conditions are favorable for a raging storm, why not prepare? I truly believe that there should be clear directions, instructions, and definitions of online classes, what online classes entail for students, what students should expect taking an online class, and where students should go once they are enrolled in their online courses immediately after they log into class. Too often, enrollment advisors are anxious to register students for online courses and do not provide adequate information and a visual representation of distance learning—or maybe they do not have a visual representation to provide to students. Students, myself included when I attended classes online, do not understand the amount of class time and extensive reading that is required to be successful in e-learning.

I cannot fully articulate the underestimated expectations for reading that some students have taking e-courses. I had a student comment that his eyes were hurting because there was too much material to read. I was glad he was actually reading the material even though I did not need to know the information regarding his eyes. There should be a mandate that students have to read before entering online classes. I suggest this mandate be included in a prescreening distance education exam. The reason I believe that this is important is because I have received countless e-mails from students checking on their grades during the last week of class because they had not read an announcement in class or an e-mail from me requesting them to check their grades frequently throughout the term. Some students request to make up assignments because they did not read the syllabus and did not read reminder e-mails from me in order to find out when their projects, particularly final projects, were due. Then there are students who do not read all the information about academic dishonesty, school policies and procedures, types of resources available, such as writing and math labs, or even information about how to use the online library. Students need to *read, read, read* everything in class.

A faculty trainer once informed me that instructors really do not know if students read or not and I was basing my opinions regarding the lack of reading by students on assumptions. I wanted to tell him to get real. If students read the material, they would follow instructions, and if they had questions, they would more than likely ask them at some point in the class. It is clear from some of the papers I have graded and some of the bizarre e-mails I have received that there is a lack of reading by students. Students should read the announcements, instructor e-mails, the assignment instructions, the course information, every item, and every folder in class. This might be overwhelming, especially if the information is not presented in a seamless format. If information is scattered about, students do not know where to go and what to read first. I have noticed online that there is a lack of conformity with the items for some online courses. It helps when students know where to go to access course materials.

Some schools provide students with a distance education introductory test during orientation or on their Web sites so they can familiarize themselves with certain terms and items in online classes. I have not noticed an emphasis on the amount of reading needed to be successful as an online student. I have designed an orientation preparatory packet that consists of three main components, as you will see next. The general "Is Distance Education Right for You?" type tests are not sufficient for students to assess whether this type of learning is right for them. Perhaps the credibility of online courses would increase if administrators demanded higher criteria for enrolling in online classes. It is a privilege to engage in e-learning. Therefore, certain requirements should be set and met for participants. I am in no way suggesting that students should be turned down if they desire to attend school online, but they should have to complete a somewhat rigorous process, as they would in a traditional college. There should be three parts to the preparatory package to help students become acclimated to online learning and certain expectations as part of the orientation process. I have developed such a preparatory packet, and I will outline it below.

1. *Distance Education Test*—This is a standard test, like the ones you may be familiar with, that asks questions to assess exactly what the student already knows about distance education. What is different about the test that I designed is that I ask questions regarding the extensive reading and writing that is needed online. In the introductory test, I also suggest that you ask students to write a couple of paragraphs. Writing is very important in college. It goes without saying that I have encountered students who do not write well and who are immediately enrolled in an English composition course. It would help if administrators enrolled students in an introduction to writing and grammar course or tutorial before having students who struggle in this area start writing essays. This can be determined by a simple paragraph in the introductory distance education test. If you notice spelling and grammar errors, the student should be enrolled in the introduction to writing course or some type of tutorial by your school before being placed in a composition class. This test should be reviewed by a qualified staff member, and the information should be provided to the student's advisor or whoever is in charge of assigning the student's courses and tracking his or her degree program. Another point about the test is that it dispels some misconceptions in general about distance learning. I have noticed several students, myself included, laboring under the misconception that attending school online means attending class at an assigned time. I am not sure why, but it is true. The concepts of logging on anytime to class, submitting assignments by the due dates, and meeting attendance requirements are ambiguous. The introductory test might provide guidance in these grey areas.

2. *Steps for Success*—The steps for success should be an activity that explains where students can locate important information about the class. You could name this component anything you prefer. This could be in the form of an activity such as a scavenger hunt, puzzle, and/or games such as tic-tac-toe, jeopardy, or bingo. There is software available that can create games such as Articulate Presenter and StudyMate Author that do not require programming experience. This is another tool that will help students become acclimated to distance education before taking an actual online class. It is also another component that the advisor could provide to the student by

having the student click on a simple link to a Web site that takes the student directly to the activity provided by the school.

3. *Distance Education Demo*—This is the most important component that should be added to orientation or for a potential student. A simulation that can be scripted on software such as Adobe Captivate should be created to show students exactly what they will see upon entering the online classroom. A distance education demo may be an excellent teaching tool for explaining terms students will use in the online environment. This is another component that can be placed on the school's Web site or a Web site address sent to the student so that he/she can click on it and take the demo.

Following is an example of a distance education preparatory packet.

Part 1

Preparatory Packet—Distance Education Test

You can add these questions to your school's current test or use them if your school does not currently have a preparatory test. You can add feedback to the incorrect questions if you prefer to clarify more information.

Are you a candidate for online classes?

Take this test to find out for sure.

Step A

1. What is the definition of distance education?
    a. Distance education is anywhere learning takes place using a computer and an Internet connection.
    b. Distance education is learning how to design courses.
    c. Distance education is a degree program.

Answer: a

2. What do I need to take an online class?
    a. A computer and Internet access
    b. The school's textbooks and online instructor
    c. All of the above

Answer: c

3. What does it mean to take an online class?
   a. I will have to read a lot of material, respond to discussion questions, and interact with other students and my instructor.
   b. I have to attend class at assigned times. All students have to log in at a certain time.
   c. I will have to respond to my instructor only and submit assignments.

Answer: a

4. What is the difference between online classes and traditional classes?
   a. Online classes are easier because the work is not as extensive as it is in traditional classes.
   b. Online classes are accomplished using a computer and the Internet. The classes are specifically designed for an electronic format.
   c. Online classes do not have an instructor.

Answer: b

5. What do I expect to learn from distance education?
   a. I will learn as much as I would learn in a traditional classroom and possibly more due to high interaction with other students.
   b. I will not learn as much as I would in a traditional classroom because the classes are condensed.
   c. I will learn how to engage in distance education.

Answer: a

6. How will my learning style help or hinder taking online classes?
   a. If I am a visual learner, I can read the material and understand. If I am a tactile learner, I will have the opportunity to complete tasks to learn. If I am an auditory learner, I will have the opportunity to listen to lectures and instructors. Therefore, the answer is that my learning style, whatever it is will help me in distance education.
   b. If I am a visual learner, distance education will be an ideal type of teaching. If I am a tactile learner then I can forget it because the instructor will tell me what I need to do and I will be lost.

If I am an auditory learner, I will be confused because there is no audio. Therefore, my learning style might hinder distance education.

   c. I have no idea if it will help or hurt. I am not sure about my learning style. Perhaps I will discover my learning style online.

Answers: a or c

7. Will I have to work independently online?

   a. For the most part I will have to work with my instructor step by step. He/she will inform me on what I should do. Therefore, I will wait for the online instructor.

   b. For the most part, I will work as a group. I have to log into class during assigned times and respond to students who respond to me.

   c. For the most part I will have to work independently and possibly in group assignments. I can log into class anytime as long as I submit my work by the assigned due dates.

Answer: c

8. How important is reading in online classes?

   a. Reading is important, but I can scan the material and know what is expected.

   b. Reading is extremely important online. I will not pass online classes if I do not read.

   c. Reading is a minimal requirement online.

Answer: b

9. How important are writing skills in online classes?

   a. Writing is not important. I will not be required to write online.

   b. Writing is just as important as reading online. I will learn and enhance my writing skills.

   c. Writing is a minimal requirement online.

Answer: b

10. Is online learning right for me?

   a. Online learning is right for me because of the flexible schedule.

b. I need more information.

c. Online learning is not right for me.

For any of these answers, you might want to link the results to an enrollment advisor's contact information or have the advisor contact the potential student.

Step B—Writing Exercise

This step will assess your writing skills and help your advisor place you in the correct writing courses at the college.

Write two paragraphs explaining why you are returning to school to pursue your degree.

Write two paragraphs explaining why you think distance learning is right for you.

PART 2

Preparatory Packet—Distance Education Steps to Success

This is where you could design a game to help students locate materials for the course. The feedback provided will prepare students for the final step, called the distance education demo. Since the student may not have previewed an actual course at this point, these questions should be easy so students can use their common sense. Hopefully, the course is just as comprehensive. Here's an example:

Play the distance education *Money Bags* game. If you answer the questions correctly, you bank the game money for fun and learning about your online classes. If you answer the questions incorrectly, you lose what you have banked.

500,000	You need to view the instructor's lecture. Where do you go? a. Instructor's contact e-mail b. Weekly assignments Answer: b
250,000	You need to research an essay in the school's library. Where do you go? a. Online library b. Discussion board Answer: a

125,000	You need to answer the weekly discussion question with your initial response. Where do you go? a. Discussion board b. Weekly assignments Answer: a
64,000	You need to read your assignments. Where do you go? a. Weekly assignments b. Syllabus Answer: a
32,000	You need to respond to students' responses. Where do you go? a. Discussion board b. Weekly assignments Answer: a
16,000	You need to check your grades. Where do you go? a. Syllabus b. Grades Answer: b
8,000	You need to determine the required textbook for your class. Where do you go? a. Course information b. Instructor's contact e-mail Answer: a
4,000	You need to determine how many days you should participate in class. Where do you go? a. Syllabus b. Grades Answer: a
2,000	You need to ask your instructor a private question regarding your assignment. Where do you go? a. Questions and concerns b. Instructor's contact e-mail Answer: b
1,000	You need to ask your instructor a general question regarding the course. Where do you go? a. Questions and concerns b. Instructor's contact information Answer: a

Here is the final step in the preparatory packet. It is a simulation where students can actually engage in class activity. They will have the opportunity to answer discussion questions and practice taking online classes.

PART 3

Preparatory Packet—Distance Education Demo

The distance education demo should depict how an actual online class appears at your institution. This could include threaded discussions, a simulated discussion question, and ideal responses. If it is an interactive demo, students can actually type their responses and post (submit) them to the discussion forum. This will provide students with insight about the course and allow them to see just how important reading is online. You may include a sample syllabus, course materials, and exercises that provide just enough detail to get students started and comfortable with online classes. This demo should show the most appealing and realistic aspects of distance education. It should illustrate messages from the instructor to let prospective students know that the instructor is present online. I have read responses from students in class commenting that they did not expect the online instructor to be active in class. They were surprised at the importance I placed on interacting with students. Every school is different with regard to the online setup, but the concepts are the same for all distance education courses. Students will need to be able to locate information and especially find their way to class. Finally, one more important aspect that this demo should include is clear instructions and feedback.

Here are some examples of items and key terms that I envision in this demo.

Smith University

Where You Learn Transferable Skills

Course Information
Weekly Class Assignments
Discussion Boards
Submit Written Assignments Here
Grades

Announcement

Welcome to Writing 101. I am your instructor, Cassandra Smith. To begin class, please go to the course information folder located on the left side of your screen. After you read everything in this folder, please proceed to the weekly class assignments folder and click on "Week One." You will find everything you need in this folder to begin class.

NOTE: If students try to click on anything else, the simulation should flag it as incorrect and provide feedback.

Good. You are in the course information folder. Please read all the information in this section.

Textbook requirements
  E-Writing 101 Textbook by Smith
  Grammar Rules Textbook by Smith

Course Syllabus
Provide a brief sample syllabus. Perhaps assignment due dates and week one assignments would depict the concept.

Netiquette Rules
It would be a great idea to include a few basic netiquette rules in your demo. This could increase the odds of students reading the material. Your school probably has netiquette rules in place, but here are some that I think should definitely be included in the demo or in your class.
  Netiquette is online etiquette. It is a professional way of interacting online without offending others.

1. Your grade will suffer the consequences if you violate netiquette rules.
2. There should be *no* profanity. This means no cursing and no alluding to vulgarities in anything that you type online.
3. There should be *no* offensive jokes. This is a professional environment.
4. Do not type in all caps for online learning. This is considered yelling.
5. Avoid using color in your postings, as well as large or fancy font sizes.
6. Do not use any smiley faces or other emoticons in your responses.

Now click on weekly class assignments to access week one's assignments.
  Good. You are in the assignments area. Now click on week one assignments.

Week One Assignments

READING ASSIGNMENTS

WRITING ASSIGNMENTS

Next, answer the following questions before you move on to the discussion forum.

     When are your assignments due?

     You have written assignments due this week. What are they?

     Did you read all the course material? If so, you should be able to answer the questions. If not, please return to the course information folder and review your class syllabus. Reading and following instructions are essential for taking online classes. Great! You may proceed to the discussion board forum.

     You are in the discussion board forum.

     Please answer your first discussion question based on your chapter reading.

     Do you get the idea? The demo can be direct. Students need to know what is expected online to increase the respect for the environment. Your school can use this demo as part of the orientation process or place the information on a CD and ship it directly to prospective students as part of the orientation process. The CD can be helpful for instructors as well. I attended new-hire online faculty training and some of the prospective faculty members were not familiar with terms such as online lectures and online activities and basically did not know what to expect in general for their first classes. What I found interesting was that some of the faculty placed written assignments in the discussion board area like novice student learners. So if instructors do not know where to go and submit materials online, how can students become acclimated to the distance education software? Therefore, a distance education demo that explains common terms and locations could truly help both groups.

     I believe these components are necessary in a preparatory packet because some students are still confused and basically become frustrated when they enter online classes for the first week. It takes more effort from the school to prepare students for success. You never know who may *not* drop a course or even may *add* a course simply because he or she understands where everything is located in an online class. As explained, the demo should provide detailed instructions and feedback for the student.

BOARDING UP THE HOUSE

You can prepare for the storm by boarding up your house. Since we just discussed student preparation for online classes, I thought it was important to place a chapter in this book regarding how to set up your online classes before discussing some of the real-life disasters that may occur or might have already occurred in your classes. There are certain elements that I believe an online class should have in order to create a productive learning environment. Granted, some online schools do not have all these features or items, but there is always room for improvement as technology changes and more effective ways of adding tools to courses are implemented.

I mentioned earlier that I am a technical writer as well. I have written online classes and training material for Web-based learning. Therefore, from my experience with working with and writing various content/ curricula, I will take you through a visual process of how an online class should be designed and highlight some important information that should be included. Keep in mind that your school's software has to have the functionality for some of these features, but you can always work with what you have until the school's administrators make changes in their electronic delivery. Hopefully, the school's online software, where students actually attend class, has some of the basic features below.

Setup and Organization

When I attended my first online class, I was lost. Because of the amount of folders and information that is usually scattered in online classes, it can be intimidating for any student. There are several folders and links to click on upon entering class. There should be better navigation for students attending online classes, especially for the first time.

When setting up an online class, icons and text are needed for student instruction. Icons and text such as, "go to class here," "go here to find out about your reading assignments," "read this first," "you are here," and "go there next," as you might have noticed in the demo preview, are helpful navigational terms. As for the elements needed in class, here are some suggestions:

ANNOUNCEMENTS

This area is for special messages from you as the instructor. You can update them daily or weekly depending on what you need to say to students. Here are some examples of announcements.

Announcement: Welcome to ENG100—English Composition I. My name is Cassandra Smith, and I will be your instructor for this class. Always check the *Announcements* when you first log into class for special messages/instructions from me. Please go to the *Instructor Office* link located on the right side of your screen and read my biography, as well as information regarding my contact information and office hours.

Announcement: As you begin writing your rough draft for the persuasive essay, please keep in mind that this paper should be in simple citation format. You can refer to the information that I e-mailed or the information that I placed in the writing corner thread for assistance. Please contact me if you have any questions.

Announcement: There should be no profanity or alluding to vulgarities in your responses. If you do this, your submissions will be automatically removed and you will not receive any points for the week for your work. Please review the online netiquette rules in the course information folder.

Announcement: January McBride, please contact your instructor immediately.

Announcement: Your final exam is due tomorrow at midnight Central Standard Time. All exams must be submitted on time—no exceptions.

GO TO CLASS

The "go to class" icon should be large, since students will click on it to begin class. Even if everything else is ambiguous online, a student should be able to find his or her way to class to access course material and participate in class. An example of a welcome message follows:

> *Welcome to your first day of class. You are in the correct place to begin this course. To the left, you will find numbered folders. Please click on them in numerical order and read the instructions to proceed throughout this course. You will follow the same steps each week to access class material.*

It would be ideal for folders to be numbered in your online class. This will provide a systematic flow for students, but most of the time the information is not numbered, it is just there. Even if the folders are only numbered for the first week, at least students could acclimate to the class at higher levels.

COURSE INFORMATION

The course information folder should include material about the course, such as the syllabus, netiquette rules, computer requirements, grading rubrics (to be discussed in the "Assessment Hanging on the Edge" chapter), and the school's policies regarding academic dishonesty and plagiarism.

Syllabus

The syllabus is your course guide for students. Here is an example that you can use in your classes if you need any ideas or help developing a syllabus.

> Name of Course
> Instructor Information
> E-mail:
> Office hours:

This is a good disclaimer to place in your syllabus:

Your instructor has twenty-four hours to respond to your e-mail. He or she is not required to be online twenty-four hours a day, seven days a week. You can send a private e-mail to your instructor or submit a question in the assigned area in class. Keep in mind that if you post your question in class, all students can read it.

> Required Textbooks
> Course Description and Outcomes
> Online Weekly Schedule

You can include a chart (see the example below) for each weekly assignment and due dates or omit this information and place only the school's academic week here, should you elect for a brief syllabus.

> Attendance Requirements
> Participation Requirements
> Grading Scale

Assignments
    Where to Submit Assignments
    Discussion Board Requirements
You may also want to place your perspective on good, quality discussion board responses in this location.

Written Assignments

Brief Assignment Points and Calendar (see my example below)

Late Policy

Academic Dishonesty Policies and Procedures
Here you can discuss the school's plagiarism policy, such as information regarding copying off the Internet or having a spouse, relative, or friend do assignments—which is still considered an offense online that is often not stated directly in the school's policies, and any other information that must be directly stated regarding plagiarism and honor codes.

Assignment Calendar

Mon	Tues	Wed	Thur	Fri	Sat	Sun
		Week 1 Begins— Day 1 Introduc- tion Response due 2 points		Student initial response to the discussion questions is due Day 3 5 points		Student responses to other students are due. Day 5 5 points
	Narrative Essay Due 10 points Day 7	Week 2 Begins— Day 1		Student initial response to the discussion questions is due Day 3 5 points		Student responses to other students are due. Day 5 5 points

Mon	Tues	Wed	Thur	Fri	Sat	Sun
	Written Proposal Due 5 points Day 7	Week 3 Begins— Day 1		Grammar Exam 3 points Student initial response to the discussion questions is due Day 3 5 points		Student responses to other students are due. Day 5 5 points
	Comparison and Contrast Essay 10 points Day 7	Week 4 Begin—Day 1		Student initial response to the discussion questions is due Day 3 5 points		Student responses to other students are due. Day 5 5 points
	Day 7	Week 5 Begins— Day 1		Student initial response to the discussion questions is due Day 3 5 points		Student responses to other students are due. Day 5 5 points
	Final Exam 10 points Day 7	Week 6 Begins— Day 1		Student initial response to the discussion questions is due Day 3 5 points		Student responses to other students are due. Day 5 5 points

Lectures

Some online schools require instructors to write weekly lectures or reports, even if the course is prewritten. There is software available that enables you to add audio to PowerPoint presentations and embed quizzes directly in the presentation. Software programs such as Articulate Presenter and Adobe Captivate have some of these capabilities. This is your time to educate students about the topic for the week. I have always liked storytelling, even in traditional settings, to begin a lecture. It usually gains the students' attention. You can provide case studies in your lectures and then explain how it relates to your topic. Or you can write a traditional lecture that is factual and precise with regard to the topic.

The main aspect of a lecture is to include pertinent information that will help the student. It should preferably be information that is not repetitive of the textbook but that has been gained from your experience and research. It is okay to highlight or expand upon information in the textbook, but you might want to use this opportunity to provide students with more ideas and concepts, or even a different way of thinking. For example, if you are teaching a business course, you could lecture about business careers and options available upon graduating. Or you could discuss new technology that is available in business or the discipline that you are teaching that has made jobs easier. Discuss some challenges in the discipline that could help students with their job searches or evoke them to search out new careers in their degree programs. From my teaching experience and reading students' comments, this is what students truly want to know: What can I do with my degree? How is this course material going to advance my degree? What can I take away from this course? Whatever you decide to use as your lecture material, let it be a teachable moment. Here are snippets of ways that I have started my lectures.

ENGLISH COMPOSITION

My Love Is in the Details
I have heard it said before that the love is in the details. I believe this statement applies to writing as well. This week you will learn about essay development with regard to descriptive writing. Have you ever read a piece of work that literally made you want to be in the scene? Or the details are so palpable that you recognize the smell or feel the raw emotions that accompany the text? If so, the writer has successfully captivated you as the audience. The writer has successfully used descriptive writing to his or her advantage. The writer paid attention to what he or she saw and what he or she was feeling and used adjectives well! I want you to look for the sensory details in the essay that you will read.

"So We Talkin' 'Bout Fragments." No. This Is Not Correct English!
How does it look when professionals write or speak in this manner? We are instantaneously judged on the way we write and speak. Since you are

in college, try to learn as much as you can about how to communicate effectively through written and verbal messages. You will have to write several essays in this course. I noticed that some students write as they speak. They become comfortable with certain phrases and include them in their essays. I have offered some tips below.

PSYCHOLOGY—ADULT DEVELOPMENT

Tag—You're It!

Do you respond differently to others as an adult than you did as a child? Of course! This is because you have learned effective ways of resolving conflict, working with others, and adapting to different types of personalities. The way adults think and learn (adult development) has a lot to do with how adults change and develop over time. Psychologists have composed theories about how adults process information and mature physically and mentally. You will learn these theories as you proceed in this course. Each theorist explores human behavior and learning over the lifespan of a person.

I Have My Degree—Now What?

Students, if you are wondering what you can do with your degree in psychology, keep reading. Different types of psychologists perform various duties such as medical counseling, testing, diagnosis, and treatment. Psychologists focus on certain areas of specialty. Let's take a closer look.

LITERATURE

Literary Moments

The gingham dog and the calico cat, the country mouse and the city mouse, and the charismatic owl were the joys of nursery rhymes that would make the most precocious or less lively child submit to full attention and beg for more, more, and more storytelling before bedtime. These stories were the best literary moments of my life. What was the significance of a nursery rhyme to make an adult be able to recall every stanza years after hearing it? The authors wrote in a way to appeal to the child as well as the adult. The catchy phrases, rhymes, and riddles captivated the audience. The audience was the main concern. This week we will discuss different types of audiences, such as lay, managerial, and expert. You will have the opportunity to write with an audience in mind. Consider nursery rhymes. What can you do to make your writing appeal to your audience?

MARKETING

The Grand Marketing Scheme

Location, location, location. If you are planning a marketing event, it is all about location. I attended a medical conference at the Grand Opryland Hotel in Nashville, Tennessee. This place is gorgeous. It is a huge hotel with waterfalls, restaurants, greenery, and more than two hundred rooms to overlook these internal attractions. As I walked through the corridors, I noticed the other marketing events there for the week. They included medical conferences, such as chiropractors and cardiology specialists, boat shows, make-up and beauty exhibits, and church-related activities. It was the perfect location for advertising a company. These exhibitors had one common goal—to promote their company in this exquisite hotel. Your text readings for the week reference marketing concepts and the contents of a marketing plan. Location is a top priority in your marketing plan. This lecture will discuss some factors involved in choosing a location and managing the process.

NURSING

The Oncology Unit

As an oncologist nurse, you will be administering different radiopharmaceuticals to patients suffering with metastasized cancers. These drugs help decrease the pain from certain cancers. This week we will discuss intraventricular, intracavital, and interstitial deliveries of these radioactive drugs and the correlation with other diagnostic modalities. If you review the chart below, you will see a list of radioactive drugs and dose measurements. This will help prepare you for this week's discussions.

Lectures do not have to be long or rhetorical because these are students, not professors. They should be quality lectures that students can reference and information that is helpful in addition to the textbook or course material. It would be ideal for students to read class material, but at best your lectures should offer suggestions to help students comprehend the material. By the way, do not forget to spice up your lecture titles!

Assignments

The assignment area should include weekly folders. In each folder there should be a list of assignments and instructions, such as the written assignments, reading assignments, and discussion board questions for students to follow. Also, adding a pictorial view (box, graphic, or chart) of what is due provides a quick reference for students in this area. See below:

Week One Folder

READING ASSIGNMENT
Read chapters 1 and 2, "Essay and Thesis Development," in the Williams and William textbook.
 Read "Grammar Rules Two" in the reference textbook.

WRITTEN ASSIGNMENTS
Write a six hundred–word persuasive essay. Implement the guidelines for a persuasive essay discussed in class and in your reading when composing your essay.

DISCUSSION QUESTIONS

- What do you consider to be the most challenging aspect of the writing process?
- What are the essential parts of an essay?
- How can you use descriptive words to help develop your essay? Please use examples from your reading.
- All discussion questions must be answered in the discussion forum.

Discussion Board Forum

This is your main classroom area. Some schools have two discussion board forums and some have more depending on the number of students. This is the area where students will answer questions and interact with other students. Regardless if there are one or two discussion forums, each forum generally has the same questions for students to answer if you want to simplify your class. If not, you could ask one group different questions, but the same amount of questions would be ideal. You might add a group A discussion forum and group B discussion forum or number the forums in your class. Each forum will have an assigned number of students depending on the number of enrollments and how your course is designed.

Student Center

In this area, students should be able to check their grades, chat with other students, access the school's online library, and access any labs or resources available for students.

If you have these elements in your classroom, you have the basic items for a viable online class. Next are some components that are more advanced and that require innovative technology that might help facilitate distance education for the instructor and student.

Instructor Café

Online instructors need a place where they can go and vent. On a brick-and-mortar campus, instructors have faculty lounges, but where is our lounge? Where can we go to chat? I'm sure that some of the schools have online chat rooms for instructors, but that is built directly into the school. We need a place, such as a lounge, where we can go and express ourselves without feeling like somewhere our words are recoverable. Let's be honest—sometimes online instructors want to talk candidly. I am not saying that we want to throw professionalism to the wind, but maybe we need to obtain advice from other instructors on how to handle a student or an inactive supervisor. Online instructors need to support each other. If there is no instructors' café available, try to connect with other online instructors during professional development training online or by looking in the school's directory for a support system. You still want to be careful what you say, but at least the support is there. Who knows, you might gain an online teaching buddy!

If you do not connect with other online instructors, you might feel alone. The only time that you will know that others are experiencing disasters is when you are having one—and you have to contact the school all to find that other instructors are having the same disaster.

Live Sessions

Since we want to maintain the concept of distance education, I suggest adding a live session component once a month for student interaction. This will give students plenty of time to prepare for attending the live session and at the same time maintain a flexible schedule. Of course, alternative assignments or recordings of the session could be optional in the event students cannot attend the live session. In the live sessions, there should be a video option where students can actually see the instructor. Web-based video conferencing software such as Adobe Acrobat Connect and Skype might have some of these options. Synchronous two-way communication between the instructor and students plus video options are needed to enhance the online classroom. This is not software that students should purchase but could be available through the school's Web site by students clicking on a Web site link to access the video sessions.

Labs

For medical courses, there should be laboratory simulations available for students. Students should be able to answer questions with precise measurements for injection simulations, medical exams, and specific cases with medical diagnoses. Software for online patient visits and simulations would be great. The same applies to math labs where students can practice solving problems on the whiteboard. These are not to be confused with writing and math labs that are often available in online classes that have tutor services. The labs that I am referencing are for actual student class assignments and feedback. Although the other labs are great to have in an online class as well, I am referring to innovative laboratories that are considered a credited course for the student's degree program.

Technology is growing, and I am sure that these advancements are on the way, if they are not already on the market. Essentially, online learning should be the trailblazer for advanced technology because online learning is a product of its massive capabilities.

3

Student Disasters—Must We Collide?

THE STORM HAS ARRIVED. Welcome to the chapters on student disasters. It is in these experiences that I learned the most as an online instructor. I will share several of my most challenging disasters with you throughout this book. Students are funny. They come up with the strangest excuses, post the most debatable responses, and help us grow as online instructors.

I grew up in a home where cursing was the norm. I love my family, but I had to deprogram my speech. Luckily, I am a fast learner. I had enough sense to know that I could not say what I wanted, to whom I wanted, especially when attending a parochial grade and high school. I am not sure if it was the nuns' attire, habits, or the grimaces on their faces, but I knew that I could not say certain words in first grade. That did not stop me from saying a few choice words when I became older. I thought that it might have been karma when my students were cursing as if they were at a ballgame or chatting on instant messenger with their friends in the discussion boards and some of my live sessions. From several of these experiences, I learned to state up front that profanity will not be tolerated online.

Online netiquette rules remind me of a restraining order. It is a piece of paper that someone can wave at a person to stay away when he or she insists of disturbing another person. However, it is meaningless if it is not enforced by someone, usually the police. I do not think students take these rules seriously. As the instructor, you must emphasize what you will or will not accept in your classroom. You must know that you are still the instructor regardless of whether the student tries to intimidate you or report you to the school. Hopefully, if your class runs smoothly and you are able to maintain your professionalism with the student, there will be no need for administrator intervention. If it does go there, you will have your e-mails to reinforce that you followed the school's protocol.

For the most part, students know how to act in a professional environment, but there are some who will try you, especially if they come from backgrounds such as myself and do not know how to deprogram themselves from the "bad" words.

HURRICANE ANNIE

I knew that a storm was brewing when she took the discussion board word "critical debate" verbatim. The discussion board assignment was to discuss the strengths and weaknesses of some of the adult learning theories and begin a critical debate with classmates. This was a prewritten course. I would not have chosen the term "critical" simply because of my natural inclination to write something more along the lines of "discuss your opinions" or "respond to other students." I say this because I never liked the terms "critical" or "debate." The nuns at my parochial grade school would make students debate, and someone was always upset at the end of the day. I am sure there was a method to the madness. Perhaps the nuns were trying to teach me critical thinking skills. There's that word critical again—oh no! Back to hurricane Annie—this student decided to post an e-mail to other students to initiate a debate. However, she did not want to debate about the class assignment; she wanted to debate about current affairs, such as the presidential candidates at the time. Not only that, but in her post, she also called the class "boring" and the students "deadheads." She also had a proclivity to curse in many of her postings. I removed her responses immediately. But she insisted that I was picking on her because other students had said curse words and I hadn't removed their posts. She also used the exhausted rebuttal that the word "damn" is in the Bible.

This was when I really begin to question the gap between distance learning and the student. I sent this student the school's rules on netiquette, the restraining order. But I couldn't help but wonder if she or any students had actually read the rules. I would think that most students would know *not* to curse or insult other students in a class forum. I quickly learned that this wasn't the case in this scenario.

Luckily, the other students in class found her comments inoffensive and comical. Maybe these students were trained in netiquette in their careers as I was in responding to flaming e-mails. If someone has a strong opinion about a topic and shows his or her emotions in print, it is best not to fuel or flame the response with more combative opinions. Nevertheless, I was glad that it did not escalate among students; it only escalated with me as the instructor.

In weeks to come, I read her responses in class about the instructor (me) impeding her first-amendment rights because she was only trying to answer the questions as stated. And in her responses, she would warn other students not to cross the line, saying, "It is necessary to agree in all interaction." This young lady was a rebel at heart. She did everything to push my buttons. After saying that I was impeding her first-amendment rights in the discussion board forum, she continued with snide remarks but did not answer the assigned question for the week. To a certain degree, she had a point about the freedom of speech. Some schools only allow Academic Affairs to intervene and remove posts to avoid breach of a student's rights. However, this school did allow faculty to remove offensive students' posts. Here is the edited dialogue between the student and me to protect the parties involved.

E-Mail

Professor Smith: Annie, I noticed that you made a lot of comments in the "Adult Learning" discussion board forum, but you did not answer the discussion question. As for your freedom of speech, most students understand not to curse and that vulgarities are inappropriate in certain situations and environments (i.e., an online classroom). I do not appreciate your rudeness. Nevertheless, please post one response tonight answering the question with regard to the actual assigned discussion question in the discussion board forum if you want credit for your work.

Annie: I put that response in there for a reason. I feel you are just out to get me . . . For example, Tina wrote "hell" in her response, and you failed to do anything about it. I have a copy of it for proof, and you are discriminating against me. You allow swearing for some students but not me. I will be calling the school and filing a complaint because you are not fair. I tried to set things right between us, but you want to see me go down.

It was clear that this student wanted to see me "go down." I actually had not noticed the other student, Tina's, response that she referenced. It was at this point that I decided to compile all my correspondences with Annie and submit them to my course manager. Since she was going to report me, I had to be sure that I had presented myself appropriately as well as represented the student's correspondences.

In the weeks to come, she sent another e-mail saying that she was taking an exam and her system froze and it "pissed" her off. She wondered if I could reset the test. I returned an e-mail explaining (again) about her language and how it is inappropriate in school to simply type what one feels, and I informed her to *not* send me messages with profanity or any type of negative comments or derogatory statements. She e-mailed me in return apologizing, and I did reset the test. Apparently, she never did report me to the school. There would have been no validity if she had proceeded.

What Could I Have Done Differently?

It was clear that this student was accustomed to writing as she spoke. As I mentioned above, she had a proclivity to curse and wanted to start an uproar at any moment in class. For students who display such behavior, I do not believe that simply explaining the online netiquette rules will help. These rules are posted for all students, and they are great to have in your online programs. What I suggest is that if your school allows you to remove offensive comments in class from students, remove them. If not, e-mail the student privately and explain to him/her how to act in a professional environment. Also, I think harsher regulations, such as not accepting any responses for the week for students who use profanity, are truly needed. The disclaimer about profanity should be placed in your syllabus and addressed up front. I suggest placing it in the discussion board forum in a post about your discussion board expectations or in the announcements; I provided an example of this in chapter 2, "Preparation for the Storm." I find that profanity usage is becoming problematic on-line. Given the amount of stress and responsibilities for adults, anything can initiate a great "debate." It seems that students are using school as an outlet, and this should not be. I am also convinced that some students like to get a reaction from other students or the instructor so they type certain comments to see how far they could go online or to determine if instructors actually read the discussion responses. The school eventually issued a warning to this student regarding her behavior.

What about the term "critical"? What factor did this play in our little disaster? This was a prewritten course. When you notice certain words that might spark great debates or confusion in class, or even when you find the curricula to be problematic, you might want to address this with administrators or the instructional designer. It will save you a headache in future courses. I will discuss more about this in the discussion board forum disaster chapters.

Hurricane Annie wasn't the worst to come my way. There were many more students and many strategies I learned from dealing with student disasters that I want to share with you throughout this book.

Reflections

Remembering the Storm

My first experience with a hurricane was in 1979. Hurricane Frederick slammed into the gulf coast where I lived most of my childhood. As I reflect on it now, there was nothing scarier than hearing the crackling of windows, feeling like whirlwinds were going to engulf me, and knowing that at any second the cosmos could cave in around me. I remember glancing at my older sister, hoping that she would calm the storm, as sisters often do in our lives. I was so young to hear such fierce winds.

TORNADO BILL

Just like a tornado, he blew in with little warning. The signs were there (a tornado watch), but I did not know it would touch down like a tornado. Tornado Bill occurred in a live session with students. I was asking students questions about the weekly scenario, as was routine in each of my live sessions. For some reason, Bill was having technical issues with his home computer and was logging in and out of the session. He became angry because I did not stop the live session for him. I continued to ask questions to the class because it was normal procedure due to the uncertainty of technology. Like tropical storms that make conditions favorable for a tornado, it only fueled his anger more when I carried on in the session. In my live sessions, the rule is for students to type "*hr*" if they have a question to signify a hand raise. He decided to type, "*hrhrhrhrhrhrhrhrhrhrhrhrhrhrhrh rhrhrhrh*" in the live session across the screen for everyone to view. Then he typed, "Can you listen for a second?" before I could acknowledge him. Of course, this definitely caught my attention. There are usually anywhere from fifteen to thirty students in the hour-long live session. I told Bill that I would be with him in a second and asked my next question so that the students could compose their answers and the class could continue. Then I sent him a private instant message using the software. I asked him what the problem was and why he was being disrespectful. Here is a recap of the conversation by instant message.

Instant Message during Live Session

Professor Smith: Bill, what is wrong?

Bill: I am having technical problems, and you are ignoring me. I finally got my system working, but I was angry.

Professor Smith: You were angry. Bill, just because you are having technical problems, this does not mean the session stops. Technology is not reliable. If you cannot participate in the session due to problems, you can take the alternative assignment. That is why it is there, in case students cannot attend the live session or have technical issues during the session. Please do not be rude. Let's try to remain professional and courteous.

Bill: Why should I have to take the alternate assignment? And you were ignoring me.

Professor Smith: I repeat, I am not going to stop the session because you are having technical difficulties. This happens frequently to other students, and they do not respond disruptively. Besides, we all get angry from time to time; you have to be able to control your anger.

Bill: I am sorry. I had a bad day. Please forgive me. It won't happen again. I am going through so much.

Professor Smith: We are all going through difficulties as adults; you have to be able to control yourself.

Bill: It won't happen again.

Professor Smith: Okay. That is fine.

I had quickly succumbed to this student's anger. You can determine by my response that I was trying to be calm, but I was hot. He had rudely interrupted the class, and he was acting childish just because he was angry. I wanted to tell him to get over it, "you big baby," but I could not respond in this way. Unfortunately, as online instructors and professionals, we cannot say anything we want to our students because we will be behaving like "big babies" as well. We have to be diplomatic even when we do not want to be professional or sensitive regarding a student's behavior.

If you have live sessions or even office hours that require chats with students, here are some suggestions that might help:

1. Remember, it is not personal. I am still working on this. The student is reacting to the situation, life stressors, the lack of face-to-face contact, and oftentimes inadequate technology because of lack of finances. Some schools offer computer and software discounts for students. However, some students cannot afford a functional computer even after the discounts; I was one of them in graduate school.

2. Try to conduct yourself as an adult. Someone has to be the mature person. Remember, you have something that the student is trying to attain—your degree. It might sound arrogant, but it is true. Try to see the situation from the student's perspective even if you would not act or did not act that way as a student.

3. If it is a live session, you cannot walk away from the issue and revisit it because you have to interact immediately. Therefore, take a mental break. Imagine yourself walking away from this possible heated discussion. This can help you dissociate from the issue in order to *not* type something offensive and retaliate at the student.

4. Stick to the facts. I abandoned the facts with Hurricane Annie and Tornado Bill when I said, "Most students understand not to curse . . ." and "Other students . . . do not respond disruptively." This was a huge mistake on my part. Every student and every situation is different. Just because other students understand that if they are having computer problems the session continues or not to curse in class doesn't mean that there aren't some students who may not have a mental picture of how to behave and respond online. There are some students who might be needier or who do not comprehend how to deal with technical issues. Sometimes we learn from trial and error. I learned to explain to students in each of my initial live sessions that if they were having technical problems in the live session, class would proceed. Now if you are wondering where profanity became an issue with Bill, keep reading.

Each live session is worth twenty points if the student interacts appropriately and responds with substantial feedback as described in the syllabus. Bill earned eighteen points because he stopped interacting due to his technical issues and because he was angry. He still had the option to take the alternative assignment if he wanted to increase his grade by two points; I would take the higher grade, as noted in my syllabus. Of course, he was upset with me and sent me an e-mail once he checked his grades.

E-mail

Bill: I want to know why I received eighteen points for the live session.

Professor Smith: Hi, Bill. You received eighteen points because you stopped participating in the session due to technical issues and when your system started working, you said you were angry, so you did not proceed. You can take the alternative assignment if you are not satisfied with your grade. I will take the higher of the two grades. Please remember, participation is essential in the live sessions.

Bill: There was no response by Bill. I was contacted by his advisor.

Advisor: Bill contacted me and said that you were treating him unfairly. I reviewed the transcript and noticed that you did everything correctly. This student cursed me out and hung up the telephone. I just want to advise you that he will probably still be upset in your next live session.

This was too weird. Do you think that he should have earned twenty points when he did not complete the session? Actually, his responses did not warrant eighteen points—it was less. I was lenient because the student had consistent responses in previous live sessions. However, I want to pose a couple of questions to you. Why is it that some online students think that online instructors are supposed to give them grades just for showing up or just for submitting an incomplete discussion board answer or assignment? Have you encountered this type of arrogance or sensed this in some of your students' responses? I have a few ideas or theories about this question, but I would like for you to keep this in the back of your mind as you read. We will discuss these questions in the "Excuses—You've Been Served" chapter.

Let's return to Tornado Bill. I responded to his advisor explaining what happened and expressed my thanks for the notice. What happened next was strange but expected. Bill had magically calmed down. His discussion board responses during the week were lively, yet questionable, as if nothing had occurred. One of his comments was, "Professor Smith is such a great instructor, and I am learning so much in this class . . ." blah, blah, blah. I did not mind. I could accept the apathetic undertone of the compliment. I knew that it was another inevitable disaster with this student because of the preceding events in the live session; I guess my intuition was a factor as well.

And so it continued in the next live session . . .

Live Session

Professor Smith: Students, do you think if Hanna had identified her values and goals before returning to school, she would have been successful the second time around? Also, what are your values and goals?

Bill: I just value myself. You have to work your ass off for someone to acknowledge your work.

Professor Smith: Bill, please watch your language.

Another Student: Your point was good, Bill, but that was uncalled for . . .

Professor Smith: Students, let's proceed.

Professor Smith [I sent this to Bill in a private instant message.]: Bill, I informed you and the class about online netiquette. Using profanity in class is prohibited. This is a professional environment.

Bill: What did I do? I just said ass. Ass is not a curse word.

Professor Smith: It is sad that you do not know the difference. Please do not let it happen again or you will receive a zero for this session. I am finished with this conversation. Let's continue with the session.

This time I was lenient (again) and gave the student full points and requested that he did not use any more curse words during the live sessions or he would earn a zero. Here again, even though I knew he was a little unstable in his temperament, he had good content and quality in his work from previous sessions prior to his dramatic outbursts.

Of course, he struck again in the next live session like another tornado behind the next.

Live Session

Professor Smith: What assumptions did James make with regard to pursuing a career in management?

Bill: I am not sure. But when you assume, you make an ass out of yourself and everyone else around you.

Professor Smith: (I typed this in the open forum for all students to read.) Bill, that is it! You will no longer be disrespectful in my class. Your grade will reflect your behavior. Let's proceed, class.

Bill: I meant what I said.

At this point, I realized that he was truly going to the left in this session. I had to use a feature in the class that allowed me to screen all the students' responses before I allowed them on the main board. It is extremely difficult to manage this feature and try to engage in a regular session, but I had no idea what he was going to say next. I could not isolate his responses, so I had to use this feature and screen all the comments. I was passed aggravated with this student, and I knew that he knew what he was doing. He was using this time as a venting session for his personal life. I then sent him a private instant message and told him that I'd had enough, and he might as well leave the session because he was going to receive a zero for this activity. I turned off the instant message feature because I did not want to receive any more private messages from this student. I did not want to listen to him try to rationalize his behavior. I also called my department manager and explained the situation. The school issued a verbal warning by speaking with him on the telephone. He did not show up for any more live sessions. He took the alternative assignment, and that was great, because I did not want him disrupting my sessions. I unequivocally did not want him to influence the other students' responses.

Have you absorbed enough profanity? If the answer is yes, I have too. I have experienced more students who use vulgarities, but these two were challenging and in retrospect, funny. Let's move on.

Reflections

Topsy Turvy

I remember the first time I saw an actual tornado depicted. It was on television. Someone had raw footage of a tornado that had touched down in a city. Out of all the weather disasters, it seemed the most volatile—as if it was beyond upset. Luckily, I have not experienced that disaster. Witnesses say a tornado sounds like many trains coming at you. That would scare me to death, possibly literally.

Online conflict is inevitable. As I mentioned in the introduction, I thought my classes would continually function smoothly because I was working with adults—until the disasters occurred. These students were two of other disasters to come. I often wonder why there just cannot be one occasional storm. Why does there have to be many storms in life? For some people, they occur intermittently and for others too often. I encountered another student whose written assignment was not in a readable format. She kept asking why she had not received a grade, and I e-mailed her asking her to resubmit her paper. Since the rollout of Office 2007, sometimes distance education platforms do not recognize students' Word documents. Luckily, the converter packs provided by Microsoft have helped resolve this issue. But if students did not convert to a later version of Word or save the file as a rich text format file, the document would not open in the distance education software. This was the case with this student's essay. She was using Office 2007, and neither the writing specialist nor could I open her document. After several attempts to e-mail the student to resubmit the paper and sending her steps on how to convert the file, she finally e-mailed it to me, and I was able to grade the paper, but that wasn't it. She had the same unrecognizable format for another written assignment. So my e-mails became more direct and that resulted in her calling me rude and telling me to "get a life." Conditions were favorable for Serena and me both to produce a storm with high winds.

CYCLONE SERENA

E-mail

Serena: Professor, I just want to let you know that I still do not have a grade for this assignment.

Professor Smith: You do not have a grade for this assignment because you have not resubmitted your essay in the correct format. This is the second time that I have informed you about your documents. However, I will accept your paper. Please be sure that it is a Microsoft Word doc file or rich text format file. Please upload your paper tonight if you want a grade. In addition, your final paper is due this Monday night. It must be submitted on time. It seems as if I'm e-mailing the same four students in this class, and I'm still waiting on this one written assignment. Thank you.

Serena: I asked about my grade because I did submit my paper. I don't know what happened. Also, I do not know about the other students in this class, but I have asked you questions maybe once or twice. I will try my best to limit asking many more questions about the course because I do not want to get on your nerves.

Professor Smith: Serena, this has nothing to do with asking questions. I can count the many e-mails that I've sent you regarding opening your assignments. So you may not know about the other students, but it has to be clear to you how hard I've been working with you regarding your files. It is past the due date, but nevertheless, I am still willing to accept your assignment. Please submit it correctly, immediately.

And there is more . . .

E-mail

Serena: As a student, I like to ask questions in the learning process for clarification. I don't know what is wrong with the file. I have sent it.

Professor Smith: Serena, it seems that we are misunderstanding each other. I cannot open your assignment due to the way you saved the file. Please use the save as feature in Word and save the file as rich text format or a Word document. Also, in your future classes, you may want to submit your work on time and in the correct format. Some instructors might have a late policy that they adhere to and might not be as flexible. It is not an instructor's responsibility to keep e-mailing you to submit an assignment in a readable format.

Serena: Please allow me to worry about the submission of papers for my future classes. In your future classes you may want to remember that you are teaching adults. You need to watch how you speak to your students. Therefore, unless further correspondence pertains to class work, I do not believe we have any further matters to discuss.

Did she just say, "You need to watch how you speak to your students"? I was trying to get her to submit a paper—which was already past the due date—in a readable format so that she could receive a grade. That ungrateful . . . Of course, I did not say this to her. It was sad enough that I was thinking I wanted to say this to a student. After this last e-mail, she finally submitted the paper in the correct format for this assignment.

But Serena and I were not finished . . .

E-mail

Professor Smith: Serena, the writing specialist sent you an e-mail regarding not being able to open your final paper file. Please submit it in a Word document in class. She has given you a deadline of Thursday of this week. We wouldn't want the same thing to happen as with your other assignment. I have to submit final grades to the school quickly. As noted in class, all final papers must be submitted on time. You are past the deadline.

Serena: Since your understanding seems horrible, any further correspondences that do not strictly pertain to coursework, including sarcastic comments from you, are unnecessary. I am going to report you to the school for harassment.

Professor Smith: I am trying to make sure you submit your final assignment to receive a grade. I was your instructor for this class that was complete as of yesterday. If you have a problem with me, please call the school. I'm sure that they will find that I over-extended myself with you. However, I do not have to be subject to your verbal abuse. Please do not e-mail me anymore, or I will inform the school that you are sending me harassing messages.

We are almost finished, but not yet . . .

E-mail

Serena: Didn't I already inform you not to contact me? So why are you still writing? You were my instructor. We have nothing further to discuss. Goodbye. Why don't you get a life!

So there you have it—the entire ugly dialogue between us. Serena eventually resubmitted her final paper in the wrong format and did not correct it after all this interaction. Since she did not want me to contact her anymore, I informed my course manager of the situation and had her contact the student so that she could receive a good grade for her final assignment. Unfortunately, she did not respond to the course manager until weeks later. She went through the grade appeal process and was denied. This could have been avoided if she had not been so upset with me. I tried to extend myself to her after the discussions, but it was too late. I'd lost my patience with Serena; you can tell by the tone in my e-mails. I failed this student because I was simply tired of typing the same instructions and getting nowhere. Yes, I did extend myself because I could have not accepted the assignment after the deadline to avoid my own frustrations and childlike behaviors, but I sincerely wanted to help her submit the assignment correctly and give her the opportunity to obtain her grade. Sometimes despite our best efforts as online instructors, we fall short. I felt as if I failed this student in some way.

I had an epiphany while I was summarizing this chapter. I was searching for a movie using the on-demand cable, and I heard that subscribers could preview movies on demand by clicking on the movie and then the preview icon. I had heard that blurb many times at least over two years of having on-demand cable; I did not comprehend it until this very night, July 31, 2008, as I finished writing about Serena, and then I understood. Maybe she was having difficulties reading the instructions on how to format her files. Maybe she thought her assignments were submitted in class. She said it enough in her e-mails that the assignments should have already been in class and were submitted. Maybe she just did not get it until the last minute between the mincing of words and e-mails. As I realized that I could preview my movie selections, I finally understood what I was to learn from Serena. Sometimes instructions are vague and incomprehensible. Sometimes people do not understand until they have an ah-ha moment. Sometimes the ah-ha moment is too late. Sometimes there might never be an ah-ha moment for a particular situation. If that is the case, then we (people) have to deal with the consequences until another life lesson is presented, no matter how big or how small.

Reflections

One-eyed Monster

Hurricanes, tropical storms, and typhoons can all fit the description of a cyclone. That sounds like one heck of a storm surge. Did I neglect to tell you that my college internship was in meteorology? I was working for a television news station at the time; I found weather conditions and patterns extremely interesting and mystifying.

DISASTER BREAK

Let's take a disaster break! By the time I finished dealing with Serena, I was really over it. I was frustrated and not using my best judgment as an instructor. It might have helped if I had taken a mental break before dealing with this student. I've noticed that when I take a break and revisit the issue, I'm not so tense or I'm not carrying baggage from previous e-mails with the student. Like all experiences, this taught me a lesson on how to construct more effective e-mails and deal with conflict. Hopefully, you will find some helpful information in dealing with your students as you continue to read this book. Hopefully, you will learn from some of my mistakes, because I am not professing to know it all.

4

Excuses—You've Been Served

O N A LIGHTER NOTE, online students have more excuses than a politi-
cian. Here are some excuses I have received for late assignments or
whatever emotions the student was exhibiting at the time with regard to
his or her issue:

- Can you delete one of my posts? My cat jumped on my keyboard . . .

- I cannot find anyone to interview for my final project. Can you find
  someone for me?

- I have been dealing with a family issue. My uncle does not have any
  heat in his house. I am sorry my paper is late . . . (The paper was not
  only late—it was also plagiarized.)

- I am not going to answer this question as stated because I do not
  have any role models . . .

- My girlfriend's grandfather is in the hospital . . .

- My Internet isn't working . . .

- I do not understand the assignment . . .

- I do not know how to write . . .

- I have been sick all week . . .

- I am going out of town to my sister's house, and she does not have
  Internet access. (I received this excuse in the question forum the
  first week of class. Then another student had the audacity to chime
  in and say you can go to the library—as if my answer informing her
  about the late policy and having a backup plan was not sufficient. I

wanted to e-mail them both and say, "Cut it out"—even though the library was a good suggestion.)

- My husband put me out of my house and my computer has all my files—it's in the house . . .

- I have family in town. May I have two weeks to submit my work?

- The infamous, "My computer crashed . . ."

- I am currently on vacation and cannot submit my paper on time. I will be back Sunday in the evening. So could you please tell me what I can do to pass this course? (I wanted to say, "Duh. Your work.")

- I'm sorry that this is so late. I have been in a family crisis all summer long . . . Then he commented, "I guess I didn't get credit for this, but here is my assignment."

It seemed by the last student's tone that he was mad at me because of his issues. It wouldn't be the first time. I had a student who wanted me to e-mail the class to make her a copy of the textbook because she was getting married and could not afford the book. Keep in mind that this was an online class and the school had made it clear that all students were responsible for purchasing their books. I explained this to her, but she was not hearing anything that I had to say. She e-mailed me back and said that I was not a "helpful instructor" and that I just did not like her. She said school is about "helping people" and that she could not believe I was so "mean." I think I tossed and turned all night about this incident. I could not fathom the fact that she was blaming me because she was getting married and could not take out money from the wedding expenses to purchase her textbooks.

You are probably wondering why I let this get to me and why I was tossing and turning all night; I guess I was still taking student interaction personally when I should not have let it bother me, but I was mad. I am not a mean instructor, and these were the school's rules regarding textbooks. I did not have access to any e-textbooks, especially not to make copies for students. How could I help her understand? After not getting any sleep, I learned not to take some of my students' e-mails personally when they were venting with no real premise. It was really silly. I can't believe students at times. I want to scream from the e-mountaintops, "*Do the work, meet your expectations, do the work, and do the work. Do not blame instructors for your shortcomings, inadequacies, or life issues. We all have them. Get over it and move on.*" I also want to place a disclaimer in class that says that while we all have busy lives and events that occur as adults, school work should be a top priority if a college degree is a desired goal. If it is a matter of life or death, then we can work something out. But if I say this, I would be placing myself out there for everything to be a life or death situation with a student.

Most online schools are great about placing information in class regarding stipulations for completing assignments. Here again, I could be more tactful with regard to these excuses. I know unexpected events occur and more than likely some of these were realities, not excuses. However, the work must be done if students want to pass the course. Think about it—in a traditional classroom, how often do students enter the class and tell their professors that their assignments are going to be late because they are having problems with their spouses? It would not matter in a traditional classroom. The professors would not tolerate these constant ramblings. The questions that I posed to you in the previous chapter regarding online students behaving as if instructors are doing them a favor holds some truth.

Some students' e-mails carry an expectant tone—almost a slight arrogance such as, "I did manage to login to class," and "I did manage to do part of the assignment . . ." "I expect you (online instructor) to at least give me full credit." Or this is online learning: "I expect you to wait for my assignment. Isn't this what online learning is all about—flexibility?" Most traditional schools have policies for students being inactive in the event of a death or tragedy, but minor excuses just because students do not have their work done are unacceptable. Online schools have attendance policies, but perhaps a clarification of what is expected online is vital to an online students' success with regard to excuses. I think it is time for instructors to address these excuses and not avoid them and not feel awful about calling these students out about this blatant attitude of disdain for online learning.

Why do we (online instructors) have to tolerate this madness? I am glad you asked! In essence, you do not have to tolerate the excuses. It is your class, and you have the right to reject or accept late assignments. But if you are like me, you accept the work and try to reasonably accommodate the student. Why? It is an unspoken rule for online instructors. Remember, you are special, and the environment is special. It seems to go along with the territory if you have an easygoing, passive-assertive personality, such as myself, and you want to help the student. If you are assertive throughout your class, you probably do not have to deal with many students' excuses because you have set a strict tone up front. You probably do not have many students trying to submit work late and obtain full points for late submissions, although you might have to deal with students complaining to the school or in e-mails that you are too callous in your communication approach. Some students seem to find something to complain about whether it is the instructor, instruction, or peers. It is your decision how you handle some of these excuses.

You can cut it off immediately by saying no—no to the assignment being accepted, no to making up any work, no to resubmitting a project, just no. The student did not make the deadline, so you cannot help him or her. Funny—even typing this paragraph about saying no, I can't imagine online instructors being that rigid. Maybe that is part of the problem. We work too hard to accommodate our students. I am not indicating that we are pushovers; even I have not accepted late work after I notice a student is taking me for granted, but it seems online instructors try to help adult learners, at least in my experience and interaction with other faculty.

Let's revisit one of the excuses e-mails.

E-mail

Student: I have family in town, and I am wondering if I could have a two-week extension on my assignments. I cannot concentrate on my school work since they are here. Thank you in advance for understanding.

Professor Smith: I am sorry, but I cannot grant you a two-week extension because family is in town. School does not stop because of personal activities. Please submit your work on time.

Student: (No response—I guess he was enjoying his family.)

Professor Smith: The student responded two weeks later trying to make up work. This was the last week of the class. I e-mailed the student the original e-mail from me stating that I informed him that I could not extend his work. He never responded back.

It was something about the, "Thank you in advance for understanding," that made me realize I would not hear from this student until he was ready to submit his work. Here again, how often would a student come to class in a brick-and-mortar environment and ask the professor for an extension because family was in town? It was especially shocking that he had the audacity to ask for a two-week extension—not even a couple of days. This was absolutely ridiculous.

Sidebar

This could become more of a disaster than you know because the student might argue with you constantly about his situation. It is clear that the student is in the wrong in this case, but be sure to file all your e-mails. It is necessary to store all students' e-mails and organize your e-mail folders.

For a long time situations like these puzzled me. I have tried to think theoretically as to why there are so many online students who make excuses for their work. In a traditional college, if work isn't submitted, students receive a zero with no negotiations. At least that is how it worked in my undergraduate school and for my friends as well, except when some major personal event had transpired. It seems to be because there is a lack of respect for online instructors. Why is it that some students do not give online instructors the respect that they would a traditional teacher? Here are some of my random thoughts:

- Adults believe that they are grown and they can do what they want even in college . . .

- Online learning is still relatively new . . .

- It is not a respect issue. Students in a traditional setting just do not show up for class or say anything if they cannot commit to assignments and accept the grade consequences without protest . . .

- Students think online instructors do not care and it is just a part-time job . . .

- Students think that they can intimidate online instructors . . .

- Students think online instructors are uneducated . . . I have read students' responses that say they do not think some of the online instructors know the answers themselves, especially about citations. I make it a point to show these students differently.

- The term distance education has often been defined as flexible learning. Maybe students think flexible learning means that the instructor is flexible and the work can be submitted anytime. If so, we need to redefine the term immediately. Flexible means you can access your computer at your convenience, but you still have to do the work and submit your assignments by the due dates given.

Honestly, I do not know. Maybe you have some acuity or reasoning when it comes to this, but I am simply lost as to why there are so many excuses. What I can tell you is that as an online instructor, you must be the "master of your domain," the master of your classroom and specialty. You can set the guidelines. You can always refer the student back to your syllabus or wherever you have detailed class expectations. I did not accept the late work of the student who had family in town. I wanted to ask him, "Are you kidding me? Do you honestly think that I am supposed to wait for your assignments because your family is in town? Get real!" Also, a lot depends on your personality and what annoys you personally. This class was less than six weeks; I could not have waited for the student's work even if his request had been practical. Discussion board responses should be active, at least when responding to other students. It was an unreasonable request, especially when the student was well aware of the limited course weeks.

As I mentioned earlier, this could have become a disaster simply because the student did not do what he was supposed to have done and might have wanted to vent. You may increase the risk of administrators getting involved. Yes, they will see that you had every reason to reject the student's work, but most of us do not want administrators involved in our classes unless we cannot handle the situation, and we definitely don't want to be responsible for a student dropping a course. Sometimes administrators do not support instructors in every decision; this will be discussed in another upcoming disaster chapter in this book called, "When You Feel Alone."

Well, it is time to address the excuses. I have composed a *no-excuse e-mail* that I send to students:

E-mail

Hi, students,

I want to address a concern that I have observed regarding some online students' issues. I was an online student, so I know that work can be demanding; it can be difficult doing class work, managing a career, and making time for family commitments. However, you have decided to continue your education and obtain your degree. You have decided to attend school online. My point is that I know that events will occur in your lives that may hinder your work, but I suggest having an alternate plan, when possible. As your online instructor, it is not necessary for me to know that your computer crashed, if you have family in town, or that you have to take your children to school, so your work is going to be late. I hope you all understand what I am trying to convey in this message. Basically, I do not need to hear about your responsibilities, because I have some of my own. I need you to be active in your work and submit your assignments by the due dates. I understand that unexpected events occur, and the school has provisions for emergencies for students. However, normal, day-to-day responsibilities or unforeseen minor events should not hinder your class work. We are all adults; it takes a level of commitment to be a successful student and obtain your desired goals. This is college, and technology is involved. Please have an alternate plan to submit your work.

The final sentence summarizes that entire e-mail and essentially can be posted in a class announcement, but it may be best to provide examples of some of these minor excuses or hindrances. Here is what I really wanted to say . . .

E-mail

Hi, students,

Please do not e-mail me with your excuses about not having your school work finished. Excuses such as my car is not working, my spouse hasn't worked in a year, and/or I pulled a double shift last night are unacceptable. I cannot take another excuse as your online instructor. Excuses, you have been served! Students, get real. It is time to play grown-up. If you want your degree, do the work.

I guess I couldn't send the second e-mail. Well, I could—but I like my job.

5

Thunderstorm Warning

SOME STORMS DO GIVE notice. E-mails that are misunderstood by students are going to occur. To say that your best intentions and most critical attempts to exercise diplomacy in your e-mails will always be conveyed to the receiver would be false. Be sure that your e-mails are clear. I know this is easier said than accomplished. Sometimes you might think that you have composed an e-mail that is simple and clear, but it might be ambiguous. For example, I sent an e-mail to students requesting that they make sure they were responding to the correct discussion question. I noticed that some students were posting their answers in the wrong discussion question forum. This was a general e-mail to all students. I had also e-mailed a couple of students who had submitted their responses in the incorrect area in class but felt the need to e-mail all students to check their work. This opened a can of worms. I had so many students e-mailing me asking if it was their responses that were in the wrong area. I had to send out another e-mail explaining that the students in question had been notified. I could have done this from the start and saved myself an inbox headache. This was a minor disaster, but not including significant information in an e-mail can lead to major disasters. There is no cure-all for misunderstood e-mails because they are inevitable, but clearer e-mails can help.

Then there are occasionally dicey e-mails that leave remnants of a storm, confusion, and thoughts as to what is going on in a student's mind or in your classroom that you missed.

E-mail

Subject—Out of Class Discussion

Student: Is there any way that you and I could speak on instant messenger? I have debated with myself regarding this problem, and I cannot hold it in any longer.

I e-mailed this student to schedule a time on instant messaging; she never did attend the meeting. I e-mailed her and asked how I could be of assistance. The class was complete when this student returned my e-mail. She said that she was sorry to trouble me and that she was "burnt out" and "tired" of some students passing the class with little effort as opposed to her trying and not passing. I assume that she was implying that someone was cheating, or maybe she was just pointing the finger. I asked this student if she cared to elaborate, and she e-mailed me and said that she was being "critical" of other students. She was comparing their discussion board responses to hers. I assured her that if students were not submitting quality work in my class, they were not receiving full points. It was clear that she was behind in her work and for whatever reason wanted to project her negative energy on classmates instead of completing her work. Or perhaps she chose not to disclose the real truth after all. It was unsettling, but I did not press the issue after the last e-mail from her.

I have noticed that some students want online instructors to hold their hands every step of the way, and they immediately want a response online. That is not how it works. They are quick to call instructors out if they make a mistake. They often want online instructors to pander to their emotions and inadequacies. It is almost an intimidation tactic to see how an instructor will respond. This was the case regarding Whiney Tim. Oops, I mean Rainy Tim. This was his first time attending a live session.

RAINY TIM

E-mail

Tim: Professor, you did not answer one of my questions in the live session. Morgan asked a similar question that you answered and it answered mine as well. I hope I do not have to rely on my classmates to get the answers to my questions from you.

Professor Smith: Hi, Tim,

      I am sorry that I overlooked your question. This was a huge class this evening. To answer your question, you should respond to a total of four students. The information is in the syllabus. I also want to encourage you to e-mail me in the event that it happens again during the session. I make mistakes. I cannot promise you that I will not overlook a question, but you do have my e-mail and instant messaging contact information. I can only do my best as I am sure that you will do in your work.

Tim: I understand that having a lot of students will sometimes lead to this . . . I take the session seriously. Online learning is impersonal enough, and I want to be sure I do not go unnoticed.

What I really wanted to say was that he needed to read the syllabus and stop whining about me not answering his question. It reinforces my premise that students do not read the material. Okay, I am not jaded. I really do love online learning. I simply want to share my disasters with my fellow online instructors.

      Another online instructor informed me that all students online might not have genuine motives in a classroom and like to rebel just because they have no one else to release their frustrations. This resonated, and I immediately became reflective of how students take different approaches in their interaction with me and other students online. Ideally, we instructors want to think that all students are enrolled for the degree and are genuinely good, but this is not always realistic. You can take notice in your own surroundings or at work and see how people try to manipulate or are inclined to bring confusion to get what they want. Some students try to push instructors' buttons when they are not satisfied with their grades: guard yourself, watch your e-mails, and be careful. This type of motive is not something I look for in my students, but every now and then it rears its ugly head. The student tries to make you feel as if you did something wrong or that you are not teaching the class properly. It is not a reflection on you. The student might simply be an angry and/or manipulative person. It could be the result of more communication barriers online. You do not have to be paranoid about students' motives, but be cognizant that not everyone is nice.

Reflections

Tears

When it simply rains without all the accompanying winds, lighting, and flooding, rain can be peaceful. There is solitude in the raindrops—a place that is not often found in the era of technology.

Severe Lighting

Lighting is never friendly during a thunderstorm. There are some students who are too nice. They are so nice that I wonder if they are trying to ask me out on a date. One student first struck up a conversation in an e-mail asking about another student's inadequate response. I sent the usual e-mail that he should be concerned with his work and that I appreciated the observation, but I would take care of it. He started sending me e-mails regularly. He said that he read my biography in class and wanted to know more about my degrees. He was very smart. The way he constructed his e-mails were not an obvious flirtation. He would include a question about the course but more questions about my life. This made me leery about posting my biography in class. I still do because it is a school requirement—but I am more cognizant of what I divulge about myself. However, I still do not feel comfortable with posting a biography because of this interaction. He also sent pictures of himself at work. I guess he thought I would be interested. I always kept e-mails professional with him and responded with answers about the course and not anything about myself. I simply ignored his personal questions about my life. I did make it clear that the information in my biography is just that. I told him that I did not care to discuss any of my interests with students, only course-related problems or concerns. He in turn e-mailed and said that he understood. I even think he tried to enroll in another course of mine.

It was a first-time, weird experience online with a student. I am glad it did not escalate. I managed to handle it professionally. If you are ever in this situation and find that it is difficult for you to manage, you can definitely inform your administrators. I prefer the direct approach. I did not have a problem telling this student that he was borderline harassing me in a diplomatic way. Actually, I do not have a problem telling any student to cut it out because there will be no online, freaky activity in my class. But I think I handled this situation well. I kept a record of our correspondences and would have exposed him if necessary.

Reflections

Lights in the sky

   I asked my husband what he thinks about lighting, and he said he thinks it hurts. He never reacts when the bolts go across the sky or the car windowpane. I recoil every time.

6

Rocky Roads—Grade Appeals

ROCKY ROADS CAN POTENTIALLY cause problems for your car. They can cause you to have to pay for really expensive repairs. Grade appeals where the academic resolution manager has to get involved are potential disasters. Most of the time, grade appeals are initiated by students because they do not check their grades until after the class is complete, they misunderstood instructions, and/or they were not reading instructors' e-mails and therefore, they blame the instructor because they did not read the e-mail or instructions in class. Occasionally, they are initiated as a result of an instructor's oversight. When incidents such as these occur, all you can do is be sure that your class is in order and that you have followed through with e-mail reminders and announcements confirming to students to check their grades for discrepancies. Of course, if you overlooked a student's response and did not give him or her proper credit for an assignment, you will have to adjust the grade. But usually, if a student has missed vital instructions in an assignment, resulting in a poor grade, then you will have your correspondences in order in the appeal process. An e-mail filing system can help and will allow you to archive your responses so that if you have to retrieve any interaction with a student, it is easily accessible.

One grade appeal disaster that I do want to discuss occurred when one of my students said she did not receive enough feedback from the writing specialist or me regarding her written assignments. It is great to have an assistant to help with grading, but as an instructor you are sometimes out of the loop with the grading process and students' written assignments if you do not have to grade the actual assignment. This was the case with this student. I sent e-mail notifications regarding written assignment preparation in my "What You Need to Know" e-mail. This e-mail, which you will review later, basically goes over some important rules for written assignments that will help with grades. Unfortunately, this student e-mailed me about her written assignments after the class was complete, so I could not help her with her grade appeal, and it was denied. If you do have an assistant in your class helping you grade written assignments, be sure to request a weekly status of students' grades and updates on any student issues. Also, send an e-mail to students letting them know that if they have problems concerning grades to e-mail you. You do not want to undermine the assistant, but in a tactful way, explain to students that it will benefit them if they review their grades and provide feedback to you if they are not receiving enough guidance from the assistant and you as the instructor. It is important for students to know that they need to make the most out of their college learning experiences. You can copy the assistant on the e-mail so that everyone is happy, if that were possible.

Usually, you have to grade your own students' assignments, so you might not have another staff member involved. However, if you do have a lot of students enrolled in your class and you are lucky enough to have an assistant, try to stay abreast on assignment grading and student issues even if it is not part of your daily tasks.

7

Seismic Waves

EARTHQUAKES PRODUCE SEISMIC WAVES. I wish I could say that I have become the "master of my domain" and that I handle every student disaster professionally. I wish I could say that I have my classroom under control and that I do not take all student e-mails personally and that there are no seismic waves after the quake. Unfortunately, I cannot say that all is well. I am a work in progress. I must admit that I have improved tremendously from where I started. As I was writing this book, I was struggling with student disasters. I wanted to react to many of them, and sometimes I did with certain unnecessary words and comments. As you might have concluded by now, I did not always use my best judgment or the best choice of words.

This next disaster I'm going to discuss really made me angry. I thought I'd heard all the excuses, but this one took the cake, if there was a cake to be taken. This student took the term "flexibility" to a new level. This happened after I wrote about flexibility seeming to be synonymous with the term distance education and how flexibility may need to be omitted from the distance education definition, or at least tweaked a little, in my "Excuses—You've Been Served" chapter. Seriously, I would not want to omit the term flexibility when defining distance education, but I would like to dress it up a little! The interaction with this disaster was not as extensive as Hurricane Annie, but I believe that I was on the borderline of being discharged from the school because I really wanted to tell this student to go sell crazy to someone else.

One evening in my prayer time, I had just prayed the following: God, please give me a spirit of humility when interacting with my students—

the one that I had when I first started teaching. You have blessed me with this great job, and I want to make you proud.

As soon as I arose from my knees and went to check my e-mails, I read the following from Earthquake Janice.

EARTHQUAKE JANICE

E-mail

Janice: To the writing specialist:

I submitted my essay in the comment section in class. I had to copy and paste it because I am having computer problems. However, I just logged in today and noticed that I was past the deadline. I have discussed this with Professor Smith because I don't log in at the same time every week. Today is my first day of checking my e-mail and logging into school for this week, and because I am in compliance with the attendance policy, I don't feel that I should receive late points for my submission.

Professor Smith: Hi, Janice. I am questioning the e-mail that you sent to the writing specialist. You have not discussed anything with me about you logging into the system, so there is no validity in you saying that you "discussed this with Professor Smith." I am disappointed that you would use not logging in regularly because you had already met attendance requirements as an excuse for your essay being late. Furthermore, you do not copy a paper in the comment area in class— no exceptions. This is unacceptable. It is not proper citation style. Your paper is late. You are fully aware that it is past due, and you have to accept the consequences. Do not e-mail me any papers. It should go in class. Submit your paper in the written assignment area, the proper way, immediately.

Janice (This message was in all caps.): *I cannot stress this enough. I think you are so prepared to turn down my late paper that you cannot understand what I am asking you. The attendance policy explains that I am to log into class twice a week. There is no written rule mandatory for uploading my assignments, so I believe that I can copy it in the comment area and should not receive late points.*

Professor Smith: As I explained in my previous e-mail, submit your essay in class immediately in a Word document if you want to receive any points. It will still be subject to late penalties. Please see the late policy in class. You can scream at me by using all caps as much as you like; it does not change the fact that the rules apply. If you submit your paper this evening, you will avoid the specialist not accepting the essay at all. As for me, I will not intervene and grade any late papers, especially for a rude student such as yourself.

Janice: Using all capital letters is not me yelling at you. I was just too lazy to turn it off. I'm not rude, and my paper is not late. If you can supply me with a rule that states you have to upload assignments and not type them in the comment area then I will take a late grade. But if you can't, then my assignment was turned in on time. Like I have said three times already, per the attendance policy, I am not required to log in at certain times. Today, I logged in for the first time this week and was informed that I had a deadline to resubmit an assignment that I already submitted in the comment area. How was I supposed to know of a deadline if I am not required to log in at a certain time?

Professor Smith: The rule is that all papers must be submitted in proper citation format. If you look at the sample document in class, as I have instructed in class several times, you would know that you should not copy a paper in the comment area. You completed other essays in this course correctly, so I know that you know this is incorrect. As for you attendance, I know you are not required to log in every day, but surely you cannot blame the school, instructor, or writing specialist because you did not log into class and check on your work. All of your excuses sound like the ramblings of a student who does not want to take responsibility for her actions. This is just another sign of where you are lacking or as you commented about the *caps,* being "lazy." I could rebut each of your points, but apparently you do not want to understand the rules. However, I have a strong feeling that you know better; you know not to copy a paper in the comment area. The writing specialist gave you the opportunity to resubmit the paper actually without late deductions. If you would not have made so many excuses, all of this could have been avoided. Nevertheless, I am here to help you. Once you submit your essay, I will grade it. I will not take off any late points even though it is past due. I am still waiting for you to submit the paper in class. I know that you will mature into a student who takes pride in her work. It takes experiences like this situation to help us grow as students and instructors.

Janice: Regardless of your comments, you still do not understand what it is I am saying. There isn't any rule stating that I cannot submit my assignment in the comment area. I typed the whole paper in the comment area. I submitted the assignment in this manner to avoid a late grade. You can't put a deadline on an assignment without knowing when I will see it. I appreciate you grading the paper. I have said four times that I submitted the assignment on time. *Right now, teacher, I'm yelling!* You do not understand, and I am going to report you to the school.

Professor Smith: Please contact the school. I would probably obtain great reviews for grading the paper of such a rude student who clearly has no respect for her work or her instructor. If you type or paste another paper in the comment area, since you know that this is not acceptable now, you will receive a zero without the option to resubmit.

I failed that test of humility. After I finished dealing with this student that evening, I checked my other school's e-mail for students' messages. As I responded to another student who had a minor issue, I noticed my signature. It said, Cassandra Smith, M.Ed. Tears immediately came to my eyes. I saw what God had accomplished in my life. I had a degree. I was teaching online. My dreams had come true. I was once again humbled by this experience. I was pushed beyond my limits with Earthquake Janice, but it did not matter. I had to humble myself. No matter what some students said, even if they placed words in my mouth, I had to show them love. I had to remember that I have my degree.

Even though I graded the paper, the student still refused to take responsibility for her actions. I hoped and prayed that one day she would learn to take ownership of her inadequacies as we all should do as adults. The e-mail interaction between us went on too long. It was such an unnecessary interaction, and there was so much that I could have done differently. I could have told her to not worry about any point deductions and explained to her how to submit a paper, but she had submitted essays correctly before, so I knew she was trying to rationalize her situation. I am simply saying that I could have stopped the e-mails with a definitive answer. She might not have liked the answer, but my word would have been final. The mincing of words and ramblings from both of us were unnecessary.

My mother used to tell me that I never "bring an argument to an end." As a child, when I argued with my siblings, I had to have the last word. I noticed the pattern was rearing its ugly head in my student interaction. I was not sticking to the facts. I was name-calling. I did not have to call this student "rude." Try your best not to do what I did in this situation.

Reflections

When I was a child . . .

I remember learning the definition of an earthquake early on in grade school. The nun who was my teacher so eloquently explained that an earthquake occurs when plates in the earth move. I remember thinking that I did not know the earth was awake to move. Why was the earth so upset that it would cause much destruction? Did someone wake it up from its nap? I did not want to play hopscotch in the event that I would cause it to become angry. The earth always looked pretty still to me. Those were my childhood thoughts regarding the causes of an earthquake.

Months later, I thought that Earthquake Janice might have had a point in some obscure way. Indulge me for a moment. If students only have to log in two days a week (most of the time it is more—but let's go with this for argument's sake), and they do the minimum, as some students will do, should a student be penalized for assignments if he or she does not read that the assignment is problematic and needs to be resubmitted? Should there be a resubmission deadline on assignments with issues once attendance requirements have been met? These are confusing, subjective, and gray areas regarding online learning. If students do not attend class (basically participate) because they have already met weekly attendance requirements, I would think at some point during the academic week they would check their e-mail. I checked my e-mail daily in graduate school. E-mail messages are the main communication between instructors and online students. It seems logical to check e-mails regularly even if the student does not log into the actual course area. I would check it because of the simple fact that I know distance education is done through correspondence; I also know that everyone has his or her own mind and way of approaching matters. My way is not the Golden Rule. It simply seems logical when taking online classes.

Go Back for Them

If you do fail a student by your actions or weariness, go back and get him or her. We cannot leave our troubled students. They need us. Sometimes weariness is the result of many e-mails and students' excuses, which can become overwhelming. Sometimes we may look at one student's e-mail as the next student's e-mail, not realizing that every situation is different. I am a Christian. I am not afraid to say it. I believe in Jesus Christ, the Son of the living God. I also believe that when he died and rose from the dead, he sent his Holy Spirit to guide us. This Spirit prompts us and guides us throughout our lives. This is what I am mindful of when I feel the tugging on my heart to do something or when I need advice or when I need comfort because I have created my own disaster. Some people call it intuition, some people call it the universe, some might even call it the law of attraction, but I call it Jesus, the Holy Spirit, or the living God. I felt the Holy Spirit in my spirit prompting me to go back for these types of students, to make it part of my teaching practices.

It was the same Spirit who tugged on my previous supervisor's heart to hire me as a technical writer. At the time, my credit was a mess. I had major credit card debt that lingered from college. Although it had been some time since I had been in college, the debt remained. When my supervisor checked my credit, she commented that she would normally look at this and automatically say no to hiring me, but she said something in her heart said differently. My point is, sometimes all it takes is a day for you to see things clearly. All it takes is revisiting the situation after your intuition, the Holy Sprit, or your conscience prompts you to go back for that student. If the student is still in your class, you can send an e-mail asking what you can do to help the student pass the course. You can ask questions such as: How can we (instructor and student) both make this work? Maybe I was not my best self and I did not help you as much as I could have as your instructor. If so, I apologize. How can I help you increase your grade? What do you need? I am willing to work with you if you meet this deadline.

This is what I did with Ashton. He was not consistent in his work from the start. He only partially completed his assignments. Then the excuses started the next to last week in class because he wanted to pass the class but was not completing the work.

BOOMERANG ASHTON

E-mail

Ashton: Hi, I want to know if I can have the e-mail or telephone number for the president of the school. I have a complaint to make, and I am very unhappy with the level of service I am receiving from this university.

Professor Smith: Hi, Ashton,

I am sorry to hear that you are unhappy with this class. I noticed that you submitted one of your papers late. You also e-mailed me about your draft saying that you "lost track of keeping up with the weeks and forgot the quiz." What happened with your essay that you had to submit it late? Here is the provost's number. She is over the entire school. You can start from there. Take care.

This student was a total slacker until the last week of class. I had not heard anything from this student throughout the course except the day that he asked for an extension because he forgot about his assignments. For a moment, I thought maybe he was having mental issues—seriously. A couple of days before the class ended, the student e-mailed me saying that he wanted to "withdraw from the course." I went back for this student.

E-mail

Professor Smith: This class is complete as of Monday. If you can make up your essay by Wednesday, I will accept your assignments. Discussion boards cannot be made up because they must be active. If you really want to pass, use this weekend to complete your work. You must meet the deadline because I have to submit final grades to the school.

I guess the student had an epiphany, because he decided to meet the deadline. His last week of assignments were just enough for him to pass the course with a C. By the way, just when I thought that there was little hope for Earthquake Janice, the last week of class she apologized, and I did the same. She passed the class with a B. She was happy, and so was I.

Reflections

You simply have that effect on me . . .

A boomerang is synonymous with the adage that goes something like if you love someone, let him or her go and if he or she returns, then it was meant to be. I say if he or she wants to go, bye—and if the person returns, run.

Storm Relief: Instructor and Student Disasters

Relief is on the way for instructor and student disasters. What I have learned from each student disaster is to become a better communicator; that is the gist of online correspondence. Although it may be difficult, I try to avoid sarcastic statements—as I have fallen prey to in some of my responses. With each class, I have tried to make my instructions clearer, especially when material is ambiguous from a previous course. Repetition is important for student retention. You can highlight important information in your discussion board forums (where students interact the most), e-mail students, and place announcements in class with "urgent" as a subject header. You can also e-mail specific students and ask them if you can help them if you notice that they are falling behind in their studies or falling below expectations in the discussion forums. Even if your school does not have midterms or progress reports, this will serve as a form of outreach to students and might provide an incentive for them to try harder if you take the initiative to send these types of e-mails.

Use your different skill sets to teach in your class. Be active in your class to dispel some of the negativity surrounding online learning. If you are comfortable with your teaching style and know your teaching style, this will boost your confidence as an online instructor, especially if you are new to teaching in this environment. If you do not know your teaching style, then ask yourself some of the following questions. Also, be mindful of your role as an online instructor. Like a brick-and-mortar teacher or any other teacher, your role is to teach the student. Place your best efforts into your chosen career.

Ask yourself specific questions to determine your teaching style:

- What kind of teacher am I?
- Should I be rigid or flexible?
- What tone do I want to set for my class?
- How active am I as an instructor?

- Why do I want to teach students?

- Is my heart in this profession?

Hopefully, the answers will bring self-awareness. Use every possible opportunity in your online class to teach and recognize the teachable moments. There are still people who think that this kind of learning isn't viable or credible. I am convinced that if we all do our part, online learning and its credibility will become pervasive.

8

Student-to-Student Disasters—Must They Collide?

SOMETIMES STUDENT-TO-STUDENT DISASTERS ARE comical before they collide or turn into serious disasters and truly derogatory interactions. Luckily, in my years of teaching, I have not had many of these to go awry in the discussion forums. One student will always apologize and try to diffuse the argument. As an instructor, there should never be a time when you ignore these situations. You do not have to respond to all of them, but they should be monitored. Sometimes the topics can stir up a heated debate. It is during these times when you can post an announcement in the particular thread (row of online comments) to discuss the content and remind students how to disagree without offending other students. Or you can send an e-mail to the concerned parties. It is at this point that you can discuss interaction among peers. Here is an example of when students collide.

E-mail

Student A: I want to teach kids too. Maybe you should narrow your subject to something more relevant to teaching.

Student B: I appreciate the advice, but I am really doing okay as far as my topic goes. Can you worry about your own topic?

Student A: The instructor tells us to share our opinions. This is what I suggested for you—my opinion. Sorry if I offended you about your broad topic.

It would seem that students truly need direction regarding discussion board forum interaction. As instructors, we can provide examples of responding to other students and examples of how to answer the original discussion question; I have examples in the "Discussion Board Forum Disaster" chapter for you to review. Honestly, students interacting with other students cannot be scripted. Too many factors are involved to even begin to figure out how a message will be perceived or decoded. It is part of the communication challenge online and the lack of verbal cues that comes along with online interaction. Some student-to-student disasters require instructor intervention. It is like the wind—you do not know when it is coming or where it is going.

WINDY JAY

E-mail

Jay: I thought long and hard before I sent this e-mail, but one of my classmates did not answer the discussion question correctly, even after you posted an example of the way it should be done. I have responded to her post in class asking her why she did not look at your example. Is this a group effort? Should I be concerned about her responses?

Professor Smith: Jay, your point is valid. However, you should address the content with regard to your opinions and ideas as it relates to your topic. You should not critique other students' work. One of the challenges of being an online instructor is that students do not read. Unfortunately, their grades are reflective of their submissions. I will have to remove your post because I do not want you to offend another student. Then I will send another e-mail reminder to all students about following my example in answering this question.

Jay: Professor, I e-mailed the student and found out that she does not have a textbook. She is trying to pass the course without it.

Professor Smith: Jay, this is your final warning. Please do not initiate any e-mails with regard to any student and his or her work. I am well prepared to teach this course. Please be sure that you are placing the effort in your submissions.

Jay: I am sorry. It won't happen again.

Reflections

Winds of Time

When winds are low, they emit pleasant breezes. The pleasant winds remind me of Fourth of July celebrations with my family. When I was younger, we would get together for this occasion, have a barbecue, and enjoy family fun. Time has moved us on to different places in our lives. The winds remain the same.

I went to help a friend enroll in a GED program for a second time. He originally left the program because the students in the classroom were too noisy. As an adult, it was difficult for him to concentrate in this atmosphere mainly because he was an adult and the other participants were high-school students who had dropped out of school. I asked the representative who was trying to enroll my friend about the classroom and instructor. Here is the gist of the conversation.

"My friend is enrolling for the second time in the GED program. The first time the students were noisy and the instructor did not have any control over the class. I hope it will be different this time." She replied, "Well, honey, apparently you have never taught before. These are adults. You cannot make them behave. Your friend needs to concentrate and not come in here wasting paper if he is not going to finish the program."

Although the woman was a little rude, my friend and I thought she was hilarious. She even raised one of her shoulders and shook it when she spoke to us. This woman had a valid point. I had never taught prior to this encounter.

I explained this scenario because of Jay. He took the initiative to try to play teacher as I did at the GED program. I really did not need him to approach this student. It wasn't like his work was top of the line. I truly understood his concern for this student, but the reality is that many on-line students do not read the e-mails, announcements, and instructions associated with the class. So no matter how hard an instructor tries, students will still submit discussion questions and participate the way they want and below-average students will hope for the best. The woman in the GED program was right—these are adults. These students will not start putting forth the effort needed to pass until they realize that their grades are in jeopardy. I am the type of instructor who will go beyond what is needed to reach students and urge them to follow instructions, sometimes to my own dismay—as you see in my instructor/student disasters. But even I—yes, the woman with nine teaching jobs—have to take a step back and realize that I am working with adults. Therefore, the implicit adult rule applies; adults must play grown up and do the work.

I had another student e-mail one of her peers asking him to explain the instructions for the class for all the upcoming weeks of the course. I am not sure why this student did not come to me as the instructor. It was the first week of class, so she couldn't have perceived anything that would hinder her from e-mailing me. I had only sent a welcome e-mail—maybe that scared her. Luckily, the student she sent the e-mail to forwarded it to me, and I e-mailed the student and informed her how the course works. Also, I commented to her to ask me if she had questions in order to ensure that she received the correct information.

Students will collide. Can you imagine the different personalities in one classroom and the possible disguises online? I have noticed that some students search for any comment to disagree with online. They disagree in order to disagree—yet they say the exact statement as the student they are disagreeing with in every weekly interaction. Some students are condescending and will tell another student that his or her grammar and responses are inadequate. I have observed those disasters and had to bring light to the problem child. In the next example, I had just sent an e-mail to students to proofread their work, and I addressed some grammar concerns that I had noticed in the discussion board forums.

COLLAPSING CARMILLE

E-mail

Carmille: Professor, I noticed students are not proofing their work too. I totally agree with your e-mail. I want to say something to one of my classmates in particular, but I do not want to offend anyone. Do you have any suggestions on how to do this without upsetting her?

Professor Smith: Carmille, you should only comment regarding the course content by sharing your views and experiences regarding the subject and the reading for the week. You should not comment on other students' grammar. Please be sure that your responses meet the requirements.

The student decided to comment on the other student's work. I knew that she would, so I checked her responses. Here is the gist of the response.

Carmille's comments to the student: Zuri, I have some advice for you . . . you may want to start using spell and grammar check. I do not understand your response. This is college and it is confusing.

Carmille had more to say in her critique; she forgot to proofread her own work in the midst of criticizing Zuri's work. Since Carmille took the initiative to post the above message and more in class for everyone to read, I decided to post the following response under the same message.

Discussion Board Message

Professor Smith: Carmille, before you correct other students, you may want to proofread your own work. Please use punctuation in your responses. Before coordinating conjunctions such as for, and, nor, but, or, yet you should have a comma when a complete sentence (independent clause) is on both sides of the conjunction. We are all here to learn, and we all have room for improvement. Please comment about the topic for the week in your responses to meet your discussion board requirements. You are not here to critique others' work.

I also provided an example of how her response should be composed. After Carmille read my reply, she apologized to the student, explaining that she needed to work on areas herself. Then she e-mailed me playing the victim.

E-mail

Carmille: Professor Smith—I feel we have got off on the wrong start. I realize now that I should not comment on other students' grammar. However, you made your point clear in the first e-mail you sent me about what I needed to do. There is no need to keep attacking me. I am just letting you know that I see the error of my ways.

I responded to this student explaining that I was not "attacking" her. I informed her that I wanted to be sure that she was clear on how to respond to her peers and to not criticize other students.

I knew this e-mail was coming; it was more of my student/instructor intuition. Now she thought that I was picking on her. Go figure. Students are funny. It is fine if a student wants to offer suggestions to his or her peers or even point out resources that incidentally seem to go over well and add value to the class discussions, but sometimes the wording is offensive in e-mails. There is a huge distinction between, "I found this Web site helpful when I had the same problem—check it out," and a student e-mailing his or her peer saying, "You and your grammar suck." It may not be that extreme, but hopefully you get the idea.

It is necessary to inform students to submit substantial and quality work of their own when they feel the need to critique their peers. One of my favorite scriptures is Matthew 7:3. I am paraphrasing, but it is the one about noticing your neighbor's faults without first doing inventory of your own faults. As people, we are quick to judge others. I guess it is easier than taking a look at ourselves until we understand this life lesson. Self-awareness and all that it encompasses is a scary feat, especially if the picture isn't delightful.

Reflections

Crossing Over

I never liked bridges. I always thought that the one I was traveling on would collapse. I wonder how often bridges are maintained. Are they meant to stand the test of time?

TEAM DISASTERS

Do you think group tasks spell disaster? Some student disasters occur when there are team assignments. Not only is there a student-to-student collision in class as previously discussed but more than one student is also colliding at the same time with other students. If one person is disastrous on the team, this can lead to other team members displaying disastrous behavior. Some schools do not have group assignment activities, but my graduate school did have team assignments. The information that I will provide is mostly if you work for a school where the curricula is designed for student virtual team projects. This section is helpful because it will explain how you can interact more in your class team assignments, as the instructor, and reduce team disasters.

In my role as an online student, I noticed that the group assignments varied—some were detailed while others were limited. Therefore, it was difficult for each team member to have the same or close to the same amount of work. It is important as an instructor to design or generate assignments that have enough sections to evenly distribute the work among team members or consult with your instructional designer on developing assignments that are geared toward group work.

I was on a virtual team with three members, and the written assignment had five required sections. Therefore, some of the team members had to write detailed sections, while others wrote an introduction or conclusion for the paper. This did not seem fair, especially when the conclusion was only a paragraph. There should be multiple assignments for students to decide on what works best for their group size.

Some examples of great team assignments online are as follows:

- PowerPoint presentations
- Business proposals
- Instructional training plans
- Needs assessments
- Internet research
- Training modules
- Case studies
- Scenarios
- Interviews

PowerPoint presentations are great, if you keep the slide requirements at a minimum. If you have five team members, each member can create three to four slides in the presentation. In one of my classes, our team had a huge presentation resulting in eighty slides; that was too much for a PowerPoint presentation online. Keep the slides limited for group assignments.

Business proposals or any type of proposal can provide many sections for teamwork as well. It also allows students to be creative with their topics, and each student can become the expert in the section of his or her choice.

Instructional training plans provide variety as well. Any project that explains "how to do something" can add creativity to the classroom as well as enough instructional components for each student to complete. Each team member can actually explain "how to complete a task" in each section of the paper on an agreed-upon topic. This will make an interesting instructional plan even for you to read and grade as an instructor.

Needs assessments allow students to research, and that is a great learning activity online. Students could locate a performance gap or a particular problem and come up with solutions on how they would resolve the issue. Also, *researching on the Internet* is a good learning team project. Students could do scavenger hunts, search for peer-reviewed articles, and then report their findings as a team.

A couple more ideal group projects include creating *training modules, case studies and scenarios,* and *conducting interviews* about a topic. Each student could write an exploratory section in the training module. Students could also create case studies and scenarios as group projects and create resolution strategies. You could have each student offer suggestions on how to solve a prewritten case study or scenario if he or she does not create his or her own. Interviews are also great. Students could interview someone in a certain career field under a general category, answer prewritten interview questions, or design their own questions and present the report to the team to be compiled into a unified submission.

In the above examples, it is easy for students on the team to have enough sections to avoid one team member doing the work or not having enough work on the teams. These projects allow students to be creative as the work is disseminated among the group.

As an instructor or instructional designer, it is important to design team assignments that will provide each student the same amount of work, if possible. There will be times when this is not viable. However, if you try to add as many sections as you can, it will help when it's time for students to decide who will be responsible for each section in the assignment.

When I was an online student, I noticed four main roles that emerged in group activities that were often disastrous. I never really liked working in teams for this very reason, but I had to participate in order to obtain my degree. The roles were *the aggressive role, the passive role, the slacker role,* and *the I'll do it role.*

The first role is the *aggressive role.* This person wants to do everything on the team. He or she wants to write the entire assignment, design the assignment, and become the team leader. This person is so annoying and tends to alienate other team members. Here is an example.

Team A consists of Tina, Jerry, Pam, and Bob, and their assignment is an instructional plan.

Tina sends an e-mail to the team forum and says she thinks the team should do an instructional plan on "How to Give a Creative Presentation."

The team agrees.

Tina e-mails the assignment. Everything is complete except the conclusion, and she sends an e-mail saying someone else on the team can add the finishing touches.

What would you do in this situation as an instructor? Do you think that you would notice if you are not monitoring group activities? Tina was the aggressor, and the assignment was complete. But it was not right. Some students will address this issue, and it can become a student disaster. This was not a team assignment; it was a solo project. I have seen it happen in teams, and the other members are truly alienated even if they do not say anything, because they will take the grade.

It is up to you as an instructor to make sure this person knows it's not a choice. This person must work with his/her group as a team if he or she wants a passing grade for the team assignment. It is important that every team has a leader for each week. This is something that can be added in your syllabus. It doesn't mean the leader is responsible for all the work. It simply means he or she facilitates the assignment after everyone on the team has decided on the section each member will complete. It should be a requirement that each member serves as the team leader one week during the course until completion.

The next role is called the *passive role*. This person never volunteers for anything. He/she might wait for everyone else to respond before taking on an assignment section. It's not the worst role to take on a team, as long as it doesn't become a pattern for the same individual in each assignment.

The worst role is the *slacker role*. This person does little to help the team. He or she might write a small section, if that, of the project every time. The slacker might respond with comments regarding the topic in the team forum simply to let other members know he or she is paying attention to the assignment, but he or she really isn't because he or she does nothing.

I know of an incident where a student wanted other students in class to type his team assignments as well as his individual assignments. He contacted students individually to ask for help, claiming that he was disabled. He could have been, but it was not appropriate to ask other students to do his work. He was reported to the instructor but remained in the class making excuses for his assignments. It was a mess.

Slackers in your virtual teams might not exhibit this behavior; it may be better or worse. They may not do anything at all but breeze through the class because other team members are covering for the slacker by doing the work. As an instructor, if you do not monitor virtual team assignments, you may only see the final product for grading. How would you know who met participation requirements? How would you determine if there was a slacker on the team? Instructors, we cannot let this happen.

The final role that sometimes emerges on a team is the *I'll do it role*. This is the person who steps up and will do any part of the assignment when no one else in the team wants to work or volunteers. He or she is not initiating the aggressive role; this person simply wants to make sure the assignment is complete and ends up doing what the slackers will not do. This person should not have to pick up the slack of the slacker. I found myself falling into this category when I was a student or going to the opposite end of the spectrum and playing the passive role.

There it is. That is why I do not like group assignments, especially online. I do not like that my grade is contingent upon whether another student submits his/her work. I did not see an active instructor in my virtual teams or substantial team assignments. I think the school might have preferred it this way since adults were involved. To me, that was the problem—adults were involved. Everyone has his or her own way of following through with work, assignments, tasks—you name it. I recall another student who was so busy trying to keep a team together that he missed submitting his final paper. It was too late because class was complete and his grade suffered because of it; this was an exceptional student. He worked to keep the team on target and basically did the majority of the assignment, but to his own dismay, he lost points because he did not keep up with the due date for his individual assignment.

What I am suggesting to you is to be more active as an instructor and try to make sure that the content is substantial for group activities and everyone on the team is contributing. Try not to let your virtual teams spell disaster.

Storm Relief: Student-to-Student Disasters

When you monitor each group and see these different roles emerging and notice that they are having a negative impact on the team, it is time for you to say something to the team. It is not a good feeling for one or two members to feel marginalized. I was on a team, and we were working on an assignment called, "Social Interaction Online." It seems the females on the team were the dominant players and could not get any feedback from the male students. I am not sure whether they were frustrated with the women taking the dominant roles or if they were not making the time for the team assignments, but it became a battle of the sexes.

The instructor must take the "dominant role" and make sure students are doing what they are supposed to do in class. It can be a large task trying to meet your participation requirements within the main classroom/discussion board forums, grade assignments, and still monitor student interaction in teams. However, it is necessary to make your online teaching and learning experience successful. What should you do? Here are some suggestions that I thought would have been helpful in my virtual teams.

The first thing instructors should do is *not* provide only a simple paragraph for team assignment instruction in their syllabi. This is serious work! The instructor should devise an appropriate document describing behavior for virtual teams. The instructor should clearly state what should and should not be tolerated in virtual teams in this document. This document should break each team assignment into four or more sections, if possible, for each lesson. The section breakdown will depend on how many students are enrolled in the class. This document should take priority, as would defining plagiarism and incomplete assignment policies in courses.

Also, request that each team design a roster to list team members' contact information and strengths and weaknesses in a group setting. I would not suggest providing a home telephone number or your main line of communication. This was the problem in the scenario mentioned above with the student who claimed he was disabled contacting his team members. He called them at home with his typing proposal. E-mail addresses will suffice. You can assign points to the team roster so students can take the assignment seriously.

Next, instructors should post responses to team forums throughout the week to let students know they are present and monitoring the virtual team. It could be a simple e-mail explaining that the team is heading in the right direction or asking if everyone has decided on the section he/she will complete. I find that if one student seems to have the most posts, it can be an automatic indicator that there is a problem on the team.

If a problem does occur, like the scenario mentioned where the female students seemed to have taken on a more dominant role than the males in the team, simply e-mail students privately to see if there is a slacker disaster on the horizon. Remind students that everyone should contribute, be creative, or bring some element to the assignment. Instructors can keep a log of what is going on in the teams to make sure students are meeting team obligations.

There is no excuse for an instructor to be passive regarding team assignments. There should not be one or two students completing the assignments for everyone. I have observed team members who actually say that they will do a section of the assignment that has already been taken. Therefore, both people submit the same section to the team before anyone notices it. Guess who picks up the slack? The "*I'll do it*" person. It is important to emphasize that students should read all e-mails from team members in your team instruction document and check in regularly in the team forum.

It is difficult to work in virtual teams because students are waiting on other students to respond in order to complete tasks with different time zones. Therefore, it is important to set deadline dates for team assignments. Having team assignments due in four days might encourage students to take the assignments seriously because they will feel the pressure of completing the task. Whatever you decide to do regarding team projects, try to be active in the team forums and post messages letting students know that they are on the right track or that they need to get it moving. Having students wait on other members to post messages can be taxing. I like sending e-mails to initiate the interaction. I guess I have learned from experience working online in student teams and even working with teams in online faculty training that attention and respect is overdue for group projects. There is too much in anxiety waiting on other members to commit to the assignment, especially if you are accustomed to working ahead, as I am.

I think I have said enough about instructors taking the dominant role within virtual teams to avoid disasters. Let's move on to what I consider the gist of the online classroom.

9

Discussion Board Forum Disasters

Must the Curriculum Collide and Have a Ricochet Effect on Everybody?

I HAVE NOTICED SEVERAL factors in my classes that might create discussion board disasters. When this happens, the entire tone of the classroom might be off kilter. One factor is when students do not answer the questions completely, which makes it difficult for other students to interact in the forums. I think that some students do not answer the questions completely because there is a lack of guidance and instruction regarding discussion board responses. I have students who do not use spell check yet still expect to receive full points. I place examples and send out e-mails about this and do not give students full credit if their responses have major spelling errors. But I did not always have clear expectations for discussion boards. Therefore, I accepted responses as long as they were close to substantial. There was no discussion board criteria set in place by the school, so even if I did want to deduct points, students would argue that they met the requirements simply by the number of postings. If there are no stipulations for discussion board questions, students can and will answer questions in any way they desire. I quickly composed my own requirements and examples on how to respond and interact in discussion boards. If your school has a point range for discussion responses instead of one set score, you can easily enforce quality responses and grade for grammar and spelling errors in the discussions. For example, discussion board questions might be worth twenty-five to thirty points or five to ten points with other assignments on a 100 percentile. This provides a range and a way to obtain substantial student responses.

Hopefully, students who usually post mediocre or below-average responses will try to achieve higher scores when a point range is involved. This could possibly result in more engaging responses and reduce the amount of discussion responses accomplished in haste with major spelling errors.

Another factor that influences discussion board disasters is the quality of questions. Unfortunately, some of the discussion board questions designed by instructors/instructional designers do not incite student thought and credible input—or the wording is questionable. This occurred with my first student disaster, Hurricane Annie. She was responding to the "critical" debate terminology and wanted to debate about topics other than the discussion question. As an instructor, I find some of the questions in prewritten courses make it difficult to interact with students, so I understand students' frustration. I also sometimes want to just say, "I agree" because there is nothing else to say, as some of my students do when responding to other students. I can imagine students trying to find something to say that is unique, detailed, and substantial in addition to relating the required textbook material to the discussions.

It is important to be mindful that we are working with adults of various educational levels. Some people are not prepared for the college level, and it takes awhile for them to adjust to e-learning. Therefore, the curricula should be designed with this in mind, especially in an entry-level course. It is no easy task to create good discussion questions, and it is difficult to determine how the class will work until it is live. I find that content should be updated in courses with new questions, especially if instructors e-mail administrators about questions that are not of good quality. I know this is a slippery slope. I am sure administrators and/or designers do not want to hear that their questions are not that great. However, some administrators may welcome the suggestions and would prefer to know if something is not working in your class.

As an example, in one of my English composition classes, there was a question regarding the usage of a thesaurus. This question was awful. As is my custom, I e-mailed students my discussion board expectations, and one student returned the e-mail saying, "If there were quality questions," the thesaurus one in particular, then she would have "something to say." I responded that regardless of whether she agreed with the school's content, she had to answer the question. I really wanted to inform the student, "I agree with you, it is a stupid question, and it should not exist in a composition course." There are other important concepts to address like grammar and sentence structure in an English composition course. I did e-mail the instructional designer, but the question stayed in the course.

What I have decided to do when questions are ambiguous or in my opinion not of good quality is to ask my own question in the forum. Students still have to answer the required weekly question, but this gives students an opportunity to meet discussion board requirements and provide more detail even if they did not answer the required question in detail. This also allows me as the instructor to meet my requirements and have detailed interaction with students as well.

WARM BREEZES (GOOD DISCUSSION QUESTIONS)

If you have to develop discussion questions, you want them to be open-ended questions. These are questions that allow students to explain their findings in detail and helps reduce the possibility of having a definitive yes or no answer—especially for students who are used to doing the minimum to get by in class. Also, as I mentioned above, you can ask your original questions regarding the topic if the questions are prewritten. Students will have to answer the required question, but you can offer additional points if students answer your question or let students answer your question as one of the required responses to other students. They will interact with other students and answer your questions, thus producing a great discussion forum.

HUMID DAYS (POOR DISCUSSION QUESTIONS)

Closed-ended questions have definitive answers and restrict student responses. Answering questions such as these might allow the discussions to become redundant. Closed-ended questions result in a yes or no answer. For example, "Is Shakespeare's play *Romeo and Juliet* effective for modern-day romance?" is a closed-ended question. Most students will more than likely answer this with a definitive yes or no. "Discuss Shakespeare's play *Romeo and Juliet* as it relates to modern-day romance," is a better question. Rewording this question will stimulate detailed responses. When certain students answer questions with ambiguity or short phrases, I ask them for further explanation.

If you explain your discussion board expectations for the course in your syllabus, you can combat any rebuttals from students because you will have provided examples of how to answer discussion questions, and students should read the material. If they read the material, they will know that short answers with no substance are not acceptable discussion responses.

Helping Students with Discussion Responses

As indicated above, it is best to provide students with examples of effective discussion board responses in your syllabus or in the actual discussion forum. Even if the course is prewritten, you can post examples of good discussion responses in your classroom. A good initial answer to discussion board questions should consists of all or any of the following:

- An answer to the question with supporting facts from the assigned textbook reading

- An opinion or shared experience

- An opposing view and explanation for the opposing view

- Seven to ten quality sentences, which is about a hundred words or more for a substantial answer

When students respond to other students, there should be a minimum of five quality sentences or more. Students can express their ideas and share common or contrasting experiences. These responses do not have to meet the guidelines of their original answer to the question, but they should show some effort and make for a good discussion or display some type of reflection and/or experience in the student's life.

You might recall in my introduction that I have a background in journalism. I worked as a news producer for a CBS affiliate in the nineties. I have composed an essay about this experience and provided examples of good and poor quality discussion responses following the essay. Let's take a look at how students would probably answer questions regarding this essay.

> Twenty-Something and the News
> by Cassandra Smith
> It was an undiscovered talent that would soon be the doorway to my career. My mother suggested that I go and apply at the local television station for a job. She had declared my major in college.

She clearly observed that I liked to write, that I wanted to be an actress or writer, and that I wanted to have a successful career in theater/television/film. Since the college in our small town did not have a theater degree program, she told me to major in communication; I eagerly agreed.

While I was a sophomore in college at twenty-three years of age, I started working in television in an administrative position, and the news director would visit regularly asking me to work for the news department. I was hesitant because I did not understand why he was interested in me. I was just a twenty-something administrative assistant with minimal typing skills. After much persistence from the news director, I started working in news. I quickly moved up from a production assistant to a news producer position after six months. Just as my mother saw the light and potential in me, so did the news director.

I thought I was mature enough to handle this type of position. I had always been a centered young woman with great ambition and might I add persistence. I was never a social butterfly who had to party all night and attend every fraternity or sorority party— just some.

I found that the news staff was truly accepting of me as a news producer. For the most part, the anchors, reporters, and technical employees I interacted with daily as a producer treated me as an equal counterpart; the struggle was within myself. I was not well-read; when I had to write about headline news, I did not know what to consider as newsworthy and what would be pertinent for my audience. I was constantly concerned about the guy I was dating at the time. The days that I should have been concentrating on news, I was concentrating on what had or had not occurred the night before between us. That was silly of me. Finally, I was not confident in my writing abilities. As a producer, a person generally has to write the news stories, set up the newscast, assign reporters to stories, decide what stories will be reported in the newscast, oversee the newscast, and time the entire thirty-minute to an hour live newscast.

Was I ready for a news career in my early twenties? I was learning through trial and error. Isn't that the way some learning occurs? I only interrupted network time a couple of days in my career. Dan Rather's talking head only popped up twice. In news, it is a big deal for local news to run into the network's time. I guess seeing Mr. Rather's head twice was enough! Usually, the network would cut in regardless of whether the local newscast was complete or timed poorly. It did not look professional when this occurred for the station. Therefore, the show had to be timed to perfection. I noticed that the sports anchor always wanted extra time, which was impossible because of other hard news occurring; that was troublesome as well.

In retrospect, it was a great time in my life. I met some wonderful people and had great coworkers. I was young, curious, vulnerable, intelligent, living at home with no bills, and almost mentally free of burdens. Who could ask for more? After three years of working in news, I learned to become a better writer. When I left, I had my degree in hand and some experience; I was ready to face the world.

Discussion Question

In Smith's essay, was the thesis implied or direct? According to this essay, what were a couple of the challenges that Smith faced? Please explain. When Smith states that she was not confident in her writing, how does this relate to the audience or what do you infer from that sentence?

GOOD DISCUSSION RESPONSES TO "TWENTY-SOMETHING AND THE NEWS"

Example A: I believe the thesis is implied. She never directly stated what the essay is about in the first paragraph. She alludes to her love for writing, working in the news, and some people who inspired her along the way. The challenges Smith faced were not being confident in her writing, being mentally preoccupied with her boyfriend, and experiencing some intimidation about being young in news. Her lack of confidence in her writing shows when she explains that she was not well read. I found this essay to be very encouraging. I could relate to the writer in areas of vulnerability, especially since I am returning to school as an adult.

Example B: The thesis is direct, "I wanted to be an actress or writer and have a successful career in theater/television/film." Smith clearly states what she wants to do and what this essay entails. The author had many challenges. For one, she listened to her mother. Even though it was good advice, I wondered why she could not think on her own. She was not confident in her writing abilities, and she was not focused on the news. She probably should have read more to understand the latest news stories. I like the part when she said she struggled with timing the show and how Dan Rather's talking head popped up in her newscast. She also struggled with the sports anchor because he wanted extra time. I am sure she had to stand her ground, and that may have not been easy, given her age.

Did you notice the differences in the good responses? Just because there are discrepancies between the two responses, that does not make either one poorer or less accurate. As the instructor, you can summarize the questions weekly in the discussion board. Usually, you will have a textbook to provide assistance with regard to ideal answers.

Now let's look at some poor discussion responses. These are easy because there is no effort involved or quality in these types of responses.

POOR DISCUSSION RESPONSES TO "TWENTY-SOMETHING AND THE NEWS"

Example A: I think the thesis was implied. Her challenge was that she could not write. She should have asked for help. She probably was too young to date. She could have spent time on the news.

Example B: I do not know whether the thesis was direct or implied. I did not understand the essay. It was boring. And she still can't write.

If you observe the first poor response, it has the potential of being a great response if the student would re-read the essay and really search for the answers and form an opinion. The student only answered with one challenge, and the question asked for "a couple" of Smith's challenges. Also, the student in example A digressed by saying that Smith could have asked for help and was too young to date. Regardless of whether this is true, some general statements have nothing to do with the essay and clearly show that the student did not read the required material or reviewed it with a cursory glance. It would have been different if the student had expressed his/her opinion after stating the supporting facts from the essay, but this was not the case. The other poor response, example B, is a general statement and does not add value to the class. However, she did manage to infer that I cannot write. But what does example B know? She didn't even answer the question. Okay, I am having arguments with myself about myself—I guess I am recovering from too many student disasters.

Let's take another look at the original responses. This time we will examine good and poor student-to-student interaction.

GOOD AND POOR STUDENT-TO-STUDENT DISCUSSION RESPONSES TO "TWENTY-SOMETHING AND THE NEWS"

Example A: I believe the thesis is implied. She never directly stated what the essay is about in the first paragraph. She alludes to her love for writing, working in the news, and some people who have inspired her along the way. The challenges Smith faced were not being confident in her writing, being mentally preoccupied with her boyfriend, and experiencing some intimidation about being young in news. Her lack of confidence in her writing shows when she explains that she was not well read. I found this essay to be very encouraging. I could relate to the writer in areas of vulnerability, especially since I am returning to school as an adult.

Hi, example A. I can relate to the writer in areas of vulnerability as well. This is my second time in college. The first time I attended a community college, and I was not prepared. This time around I feel confident, and I like the way the online classes are set up.

Example B: The thesis is direct, "I wanted to be an actress or writer and have a successful career in theater/television/film." Smith clearly states what she wants to do and what this essay entails. The author had many challenges. For one, she listened to her mother. Even though it was good advice, I wondered why she could not think on her own. She was not confident in her writing abilities, and she was not focused on the news. She probably should have read more to understand the latest news stories. I like the part when she said she struggled with timing the show and how Dan Rather's talking head popped up in her newscast. She also struggled with the sports anchor because he wanted extra time. I am sure she had to stand her ground, and that may have not been easy, given her age.

Hi, example B. I think that her mother was providing insight into her life the same as the news director did. It seemed to have helped her career. I wish someone would have guided me more early on in my life. I felt very alone returning to school because I lacked family support.

The above student interaction is sufficient to meet discussion board requirements for interacting with other students. These responses illustrate how students can disagree in a constructive manner. This is accomplished simply by the student stating his or her opinion. It simply takes one common phrase or statement to help students reply and meet their requirements. They simply need to read and place effort into their work.

As with the poor original student responses, it is easy to compose poor student-to- student responses because there is no effort, just basic one liners.

Example A: I think the thesis was implied. Her challenge was that she could not write. She should have asked for help. She probably was too young to date. She could have spent time on the news.

Hi, example A. I agree with you. The essay was good, but she was too young to date.

Example B: I do not know whether the thesis was direct or implied. I did not understand the essay. It was boring. And she still can't write.

Hi, example B. I did not get this essay either. I was thinking maybe she should return to school for writing. Was there a thesis?

Observation note: When students originally respond to the question with a poor response, this can lead to more poor responses as a result of interaction in the discussion forum between students, as noted in the above example. This is not the ideal way a discussion forum should work. In these instances, it is time for you as the instructor to ask more questions regarding the topic or e-mail the students involved to have them review discussion board requirements.

DISCUSSION BOARD WOES

Discussion board responses should promote interaction among students and the instructor. Some students really desire to learn and interact with other students online. I had a student pose a question in class asking if she was part of the class. She said students did not respond to her in class, nor did I. I had to explain to this student that I was not required to respond to all students, but I did my best to respond to posts from each student during the duration of the class. I also explained that students responded to whomever they chose, and I asked her to not take it personally if students did not respond to her. I did interact with this student more as a result of this, and I noticed that other students responded to her as well.

If you have sixty students in one class on average and you are teaching more than one class, it would be unrealistic to think that you could respond to every student. However, most online classes are not that large. I just happened to work for a school with high enrollment because of the fact that the college offered hybrid (in-class and online) courses. In the event that your class is large, you can document who you respond to on a weekly basis, but I respond to posts that I relate to just as some students do. I also respond to students to initiate more effort from them in their work. It is a trying task, but I believe it is part of our jobs as online instructors to really become involved in the discussion forums.

Being an online instructor takes a lot of work, especially if the instructor takes his/her job seriously. For people to comment that this type of learning is easy or not credible is far from the truth. From an online instructor and online student's perspective, it is hard work. It is detailed work. It is creative work. A person who responds differently might not have experienced this type of learning or might have taken one e-course that went awry. A misrepresentation of the facts produces erroneous statements and inflates the rumor mill.

One great aspect that has helped tremendously with interaction in my class is asking questions, as I referenced a couple of times in this book. I create threads in the discussion board forums called, "Questions for Students" in my prewritten classes. This also aids in your presence in the course.

Here are a couple of examples of questions that I have posed in my classes:

Questions for Students:

You may respond to any of these questions as *one* of your required responses to other students due by next Tuesday for week two. Your initial response to the discussion board question is still required, as well as two responses (this can be used as one required student response) to other students. Please let me know if you have any questions.

Since you will be writing papers in this class and throughout your college experience, this question is about essay development. I will provide a summary at the end of the week.

What makes a good academic essay? For example, what concepts and/or structure should be included in a college paper?

Should a good paper include quotations?

Should a good paper include "lofty rhetoric" to depict intelligence in academia?

Questions for Students:

You may respond to any of these questions as *one* of your required responses to other students due by next Tuesday for week five. Your initial response to the discussion board question is still required, as well as two responses (this can be used as one required student response) to other students. Please let me know if you have any questions.

This week we are discussing adult development and lifespan. Since you have scenarios and discussion questions to answer regarding older adulthood and the transitions that occur during this stage, I want you to answer the following questions. If you are not satisfied with the answers, you can change today; the choice is yours.

Is my life a life well-lived?

Have I dedicated myself to self and others?

Have I placed all prejudices and stereotypes aside to help my fellow man?

Have I done my best and given my best, or can I do more regarding family, career, and/or friends?

Have I decided in "all my getting" in my adult life what is important and why?

I am sure you understand how this works. Whatever your specialty is, you can ask instructor-led questions to get the group going. If it is math, you can have students solve problems and explain their logic behind the answers. If it is a business class, you can ask questions about current affairs and ask students what they would do if their businesses were experiencing certain scenarios. This is your time to encourage students to share their personal perspectives and ask thought-provoking questions. In any question that you ask in the discussion board forums, try to provide a summary at the end of the week. This is your time to teach; always be mindful of recognizing the teachable moments.

Storm Relief: Discussion Disasters

Not only do I pose questions in the actual discussion board forums regarding the topic for more interaction, but I also truly make the discussion forums my teaching area. I find this tactic helpful for students when I post instructions in this area regarding complex assignments and use this area for teaching opportunities. It seems that students visit the discussion board forum more than any other item in class—so they are more likely to read your post there. I have clarified assignments, provided examples of how to answer the discussion board questions, provided short lecture material in this area, and highlighted information that can be considered transferable skills in the event that there are students who really want to embrace the full college learning experience—and I believe there are many students who are overachievers and love learning online. They are not all disasters.

In many of my classes, I noticed that students struggled with citing Web sites and formatting title pages. Therefore, I posted an original thread in the discussion board forum titled "What You Need to Know" and explained how to cite a Web site in text, how to format title pages, grammar rules, and how to format a reference page. I update this note depending on what is needed for the class. I received more positive feedback from this post than from explaining this information in my lectures. That was one of my good days when I truly felt like my students got it! They actually got it!

Email

What You Need to Know
Hi, students,

Here is what you need to know as you begin writing your essays. I expect to see this in all written assignments to avoid point deductions.

All papers should have a title page (see the sample document in the writing corner). The header should be embedded in your document. To do this, go to the "View" menu in your Word document and click on "Header and Footer." There you should type a shorter version of your title, insert page numbers, and justify the header to the right of your page. It should appear on every page in your document if you do this correctly.

Do not use "you or your" second-person point of view in this essay. It is okay to use first-person "I" point of view, since this is a narrative. However, you should know that most formal essays are written from third-person point of view, "he, she, it, or they."

All papers should be double spaced.

All margins should be one inch all around. To change margins, go to the "File" menu in your Word document, click on "Page Setup," and look for the "Margins" tab. There you will change your right, left, top, and bottom margins to one inch.

You would probably not be surprised how many students do not know how to format a title page or are not aware that essays should be double spaced. As I commented, this was a great learning week! And this is a great way to end the disasters.

10

I Can't Take another Disaster

WHERE DO YOU DRAW the line between being an instructor who ex- emplifies a professional attitude to just being a person with raw emotions? It is challenging when oftentimes students are rude and go to the left on you because they are having a bad day. As an instructor, you can be objective and realize that it is not personal—but let's be real. Sometimes you might want to tell the student just how rude and childish he or she is behaving (as I have in my instructor and student disaster e-mails), and you may want to emphasize the fact that you have your degree (so basi- cally, do not cross the line) in a few "choice" words.

Recently, I was trying to help a student who completed her assign- ment incorrectly. She had not read the instructions, and I informed her of her error but said that I would work with her. She still submitted the document with the original issue after I explained what was expected in the e-mail. I informed her about the importance of reading to be success- ful online. She e-mailed me in return and said, "Let's not play tit for tat . . . from now on I will follow the instructions." I wanted to e-mail her back and say, "Sweetie, 'tit for tat,' I am trying to help you. If my e-mails will motivate you to do what is expected online, maybe I should keep sending them to you, slacker."

Okay, let's rewind. You know that if you e-mail this type of mes- sage, all parties involved are behaving just as rudely and childishly as the ungrateful student, as indicated in the disaster chapters. However, my raw emotions were rising. It wasn't a disaster, and it quickly subsided because she began following class instructions. I explained this because it takes a special person to want to educate another and to want to genuinely impart knowledge in someone else's life and make the path smooth in any way. It takes a special person to want to see others succeed. And even if it's late, this special person will stay up until the early morning grading papers, explaining instructions for the zillionth time, and oftentimes neglecting family on special occasions to constantly check e-mails and respond to students promptly because there is always an e-mail from an online student. This special person will take some of the insults with a grain of salt. And even if this special person who is an online instructor fails as often as I have, he or she tries again and realizes that we are works in progress, and we really do care about our students.

One of the aspects that I value the most about online instructors is that teaching occurs virtually twenty-four hours a day. Very seldom do online schools close for holidays except for Christmas. The online instructor is constantly cognizant of students and having to check e-mails to resolve issues and answer questions.

I say this to summarize the characteristics of an online instructor, and even though a student disaster is occurring, you still hold true to that level of commitment and loyalty to yourself and your students. You are a special person. You are a great person.

I pose this question a second time. Where do you draw the line between being an instructor who exemplifies a professional attitude and just being a person with raw emotions? The answer is that I do not know. Sometimes absurd students' e-mails can initiate a myriad of e-mails from you just to clarify instructions. Your "raw emotions" may reflect in some of these e-mails. I do have one suggestion and that is to try your best to bring confusion to an end. Do not go on and on, as I have fallen prey to at times. Simply give the student a deadline, and if he or she does not comply, you did your part. Ultimately, it is up to you. Online instructors will have emotions. We are humans, but we are special too. We admit our mistakes and move forward.

INSTRUCTORS, MAN UP!

Since we have established that we fail as instructors from time to time—okay, I fail as an online instructor at times—I have a challenge for you. It is time to "man up." Female instructors, it is time to man up! Male instructors, it is time to man up! My definition of manning up in the education arena is to become the expert of your classroom. Use every possible occasion as a *"teaching moment"* so that students will begin to see the difference in online learning. Perhaps this will change some of the negative stereotypes that accompany online learning. Let students know that you are present in class. You can do this by adding responses and information to the discussion board forums that go beyond your requirements as an instructor. Basically, I am saying that you should teach, teach, teach. That is why you were hired as an online instructor. Take the time to make a difference in your students' lives. You can start today.

I have received many great evaluations from my students—believe it or not. For the most part, students say that I am encouraging and that they learned valuable information in my class. Some of my students say that I am strict but fair. I would love for them all to say that I was a unique teacher, a teacher who went beyond expectations—and I would love for them to speak about the knowledge gained. I would love for them to speak about how online education is the best. I would love for the positive aspects about online learning to hit the negative comments about online learning out of the ballpark. I have had students make statements such as these, but not nearly enough. I have some work to do—and so do you if you want to make a greater impact.

Do Not Assume

I am sure you heard the adage that when you assume, you make an a** out of you and me. It is not the most decorative phrase, but it is popular, and it holds some truth. I am sure you noticed in some of my disasters that there were a lot of mincing of words in both the students' and my messages. Each party assumed that the other was actually "hearing" what was being conveyed in the written message. I assumed students knew how to submit their assignments. I assumed students were aware of class expectations. I assumed students were aware of proper netiquette. Maybe they were or were not, but it is best to explain yourself clearly in the initial contact. Whether the initial contact is in class with instructions or in an e-mail in response to a student's question—clarification can go a long way.

We (online instructors) have to man up and teach the students. We have to explain basic instructions in e-mails. Although this might be tiresome on occasions, it is what I know for certain is necessary to avoid some disasters. Sometimes students honestly do not know. Just today, September 25, 2008, a student submitted her final essay in the general questions forum in class. This student is a registered nurse. I determined this by her credentials on her name. I was certain that she was accustomed to being detailed-oriented. She had no clue that her paper should not be posted in the main question area for all students to read. I quickly removed her paper and informed her where to submit her final. I also sent an e-mail reminding students where to submit their written assignments even though the information was in class. It is little things such as this that are annoying yet need extra attention. It is always good to be mindful in your student interaction that sometimes students just do not know. Some of these students are totally new to online learning. In retrospect, I cannot believe I assumed that some of my students knew certain terminology that I used in e-mails and in the class. Silly me—I am a true work in progress.

Instructor Woes

As indicated above, it seems that online learning happens twenty-four hours a day, seven days a week. No matter how often you check your messages, there is always a student with a request. And the salary as an adjunct is not that great. You actually have to teach about five classes in order to have a substantial income if you do not have a full-time job. Therefore, most online instructors, myself included, teach online because we desire to do so and are special instructors—we truly care about our students and love our jobs. We also enjoy the convenience of distance education.

I often wondered in my disasters how I could take "me" out of the equation and continue to humble myself. I know that I am the instructor, but I was speaking more of personal feelings, biases, and thoughts that quickly arise in disasters. I know for certain that I do not want to become so confident in my teaching abilities that I cannot learn from my students. I do not want to become complacent with my position as an online instructor and only see it as a part-time gig. Since I felt that teaching online is my calling, I prayed and asked God to allow me to commit my time to my students so that I could really begin to teach online. About a month later, I was laid off from my full-time job as a technical writer; I was relieved. God had answered my prayer, and now it was time for me to live up to my request. I have been working diligently ever since even in the midst of my disasters. I recently received a bonus from one of my schools because of my exceptional work; it made me proud. It was another high moment in my online teaching career. By the way, I still work as a freelance technical writer, but it is my choice when I accept assignments. Online teaching takes priority in my career life.

11

Prewritten Courses—Preventing Disasters

FOR YOUR PREWRITTEN COURSES, this is your time to shine as an instructor and go into overdrive to prevent disasters. This is your time to make distance education credible and prove the naysayers wrong. If you want to make your prewritten course interesting, you have to show what you know as an instructor. What is your area of expertise? Let's think about this for a second. The average online course is twelve weeks. I've taught some classes for ten weeks and some lasting for only five weeks; that's not long. Therefore, this is your time to make an impact on these students. You have a small window of opportunity. And if you love teaching as much as I do, why not show them what you've got?

If your course is prewritten, it is easy to fall into the habit of grading papers, posting announcements, and providing feedback when students ask questions. But what is going on in between these times? What tone have you set in your class for the in-between times? I suggest placing effort into your lectures and making them good. Inform your students about what you know, post messages about your area of expertise in the discussion board area, and send weekly e-mails and tips about information that you believe all college students should know to prepare them for the workforce. Let your reputation as an online instructor precede you.

I have already discussed how you can add other discussion questions to spruce up your prewritten courses. You can also add activities for extra credit, and you can initiate student-to-student interaction. In the actual discussion forum, which I consider the major classroom area, you can select one student's response and have other students comment about what was said. Of course, this takes some skill because you do not want other students critiquing the student's work, nor do you want to initiate a "critical" debate, as indicated in my first student disaster. You do want to initiate constructive, not combative, responses in your class. To do this, simply take the emphasis off the student once you mention his or her name as an attention getter in class and place the emphasis on the topic. Here's an example:

> Bianca made a great point about information technology. She commented about the security of online shopping. Recently, I was listening to the news and I heard that millions of credit and debit card numbers were stolen from some U.S. retailers by a computer hacker.
>
> Does this deter you from using debit and credit cards in a store or online?
>
> How do you feel when you shop for convenience, yet find that some companies' network security systems are lax? Please explain your answers.

Asking questions that are prompted from students' responses will spice up your discussion forums for prewritten courses. Some other great practices for prewritten courses are as follows:

- Post quotations (any from the Internet or books that you have read) regarding the topic of the week and gather comments from students regarding the quotations.

- Share your work experiences regarding the topic of the week and give students the opportunity to discuss any similarities or differences.

- Discuss a current problem regarding the topic of the week and ask students how they would solve the problem.

- Provide tips to promote student growth. You can send e-mails and post messages in your class regarding test-taking tips, note-taking tips, writing tips, staying motivated tips, online student best practices tips, and topic of the week tips. Create a tip of the week. I am sure you get the "tip" idea.

- Search the Internet. Use the Internet as your friend. Search for educational Web sites that will help students. Visit some online libraries, or even make use of the school's online libraries by posting articles that might be interesting to students in your class. This will help them become familiar with the school's online library as well as provide a teachable moment for you.

- Provide a video link. I had a communication instructor who would show movies to convey the message about different types of communication styles. She also showed Super Bowl commercials to illustrate different marketing strategies and polled students on the best advertisement. I loved that class! For online learning, you can provide a Web site that shows video clips relevant to the topic of the week and then have students chat about the clips in the discussion forum.

All of these practices and activities can be implemented in addition to the course curriculum set in place. It is not something that you have to do every week, but it would be nice to include various activities in your classes. You want students to know that you are present in the classroom and that you are a teacher to remember.

12

Are You Your Own Disaster?

ARE YOU YOUR OWN disaster in your classroom? Are you the reason why there is chaos in the class? I need to revisit virtual team assignments—so indulge me. I attended online faculty training recently, and we had a team assignment. Three days had passed, and another potential online faculty candidate and I were the only two members participating out of five team members in the team forum. The third day I e-mailed the other faculty members asking them to participate because the assignment was due on day five, and we really needed their feedback. However, I felt the curse words rearing their ugly heads because of my frustration. I wanted to say, "Why the heck [but not that diplomatic] do I have to e-mail you to participate? How do you expect students to take team assignments seriously if you won't even participate?"

I did hear from three of the team members that night, and two participated. The other one said, "Thank you for getting the thread started" but did not provide her feedback. She said she taught at a grade school and that she was "very busy." I kindly asked for it a second time. I started to think that they were not taking this seriously. These were potential online faculty members. No wonder online students think online instructors do not care, since these are only part-time jobs—a couple thousand dollars in the instructor's bank account. I guess students are shocked when I show up to teach online. Some instructors are not committing to the online teaching quest. It was not only the team assignment; some of their general responses in the training were also red flags. I started to think, *These instructors will do the minimum in their classes and get by for as long as they can until they have a wake-up call.* These are people's lives we are affecting when we are online instructors. Why not impart knowledge? Sure, I could have not e-mailed the other members and turned in our assignment as it was—but it was a group project, with a group grade. I was not going to risk it for some slackers. Yes, I was back into my familiar "I'll do it role" in another team assignment.

I pose this question to you a second time: are you your own disaster in your classroom? As I was writing this chapter, I was having another one of my early-morning conversations with God. This time it was about title pages. I could not for the life of me understand why one student was having such difficulty with his title page. Then I heard the voice from the Almighty quietly in my spirit, *Are you having teachable moments?* I had to laugh. Had I updated my lectures lately? Had I done an inventory of my classes? It was necessary. Had I tried to teach something as simple as a title page? The answer was emphatically no. I had not updated information in awhile, and I had not moved into a more efficient e-mail-filing system for my classes to easily retrieve my correspondences with students—which was needed. I had not thought of an activity in my prewritten course to concentrate strictly on title pages.

I started to think of how I could do better in my classes. How could I increase my "teachable moments"? It is necessary to do inventory of your classes and to ask yourself if you are the disaster in your classroom. Are you being a slacker? I am not writing to judge you. As you can tell, I have no room for judgment, only improvement. I am trying to help you review your classes if you feel the need as we proceed through this together. Oh yeah, as a result of this, I decided to teach title pages. I sent a Word document to all students that only included a title page, posted an e-mail in the discussion forum about title pages, and placed the information in a mini-lecture. I figured that with three locations with information on title pages, someone was guaranteed to understand.

ANOTHER RAINY NIGHT

It was another long night of grading papers. I was becoming frustrated because I was noticing the same mistakes that I had commented on in students' drafts were still in their final essays. I had to take a break and walk away from the computer to gather my thoughts. It perplexes me that students do not read the instructions and follow through with their assignments, but I have discussed this already; you know how I feel about the lack of reading by online students.

When I was in faculty training, another online instructor asked me if I was still as lenient as I was when I first started teaching. My answer was that I believe I have remained consistent, but some days are more challenging than others. I want to see every student pass successfully, so I do try to work diligently—especially with students who appear to be totally lost online and who are not reading the required material. This online instructor commented that she did not believe in being "lenient," because if an instructor is lenient with one student, he/she has to be lenient with all students. I explained to her that it is difficult to articulate in words. This young lady had never taught online before— sort of like my experience with the woman at the GED program. She could not understand the complexities of damaged files, e-mail turnaround time, and students not following instructions. All of these eccentricities play a factor in student assignment delays, especially when students have completed the assignment but did not follow instructions fully. I think it is different for each online faculty member with regard to leniency. As you know by now, I have a passion to teach online. I believe that it is part of my life's calling. Another potential faculty candidate chimed into our conversation and said that he did not know whether he was a lenient instructor because he has a "soft heart" or if it is a "practical" way of doing what is best for the student, but he tries to work with his adult students and be flexible as well. He also stated that each situation is unique, so it would be difficult to say something across the board or apply a general principle. I do believe a best practice is to adhere to class standards and if you become lenient as time permits students will be grateful.

Some students start class not following instructions, go through class not following instructions, and end class not following instructions. I would be deceptive if I said that I missed some of my students when the class was complete for this very reason—but that does not mean that I did not keep encouraging them along the way to reach their full potential.

13

When You Feel Alone

Administration-related Disasters

L UCKILY, I HAVE NOT had many administrator disasters, but I have felt alone online. That is what prompted me to write this book. I have also stated my concerns to some school administrators. I believe, although I was never formally told, that I was the catalyst for one of my online schools to show a little love to online instructors. Basically, I was having conflict with the writing specialist in one of my classes. I noticed that grades were not being submitted in a timely manner, and students were starting to complain to me in e-mails. My writing specialist commented that I might want to remind students of the late policy and that they could not expect timely feedback from him if they weren't submitting their assignments by the due date. I responded, "Please do not try to indicate that I'm not enforcing the late policy. I've informed students several times as well as posted an announcement. Also, I have e-mails from students saying that they are still waiting on a grade from you. Do not try to imply that students' papers are late when in fact it's your grading that is behind schedule." He apologized and said that he was not implying anything.

I am sure I was overreacting a little, but students were e-mailing me—and I had experienced specialists who were slackers in the past; I thought it was recurring. The specialist manager intervened and said that the writing specialist was following procedures. Then the academic manager e-mailed me and informed me about the specialist's role in my classroom, as if I did not know this information. I really felt as if I was being ganged up on by all of them after I sent the writing specialist the e-mail. I actually returned an e-mail to the academic manager and informed her that I was aware of the specialist's role, but I asked about the instructor's role in making sure students are receiving what they need in class. How does this factor into a specialist not doing his or her job? I commented that I felt like we as online instructors are alone. Where is our policy with regard to coworkers not completing their tasks and students going into chaos mode as a result? The academic manager e-mailed me back addressing my concerns and telling me that she appreciated the job that I was doing. Soon after, I commented to another administrator about the lack of online faculty support and initiatives. Again, this comment was followed by another e-mail with apologies from the school and great appreciation for my work. I wasn't looking for someone to pander my emotions or confirm my work ethic in this situation; I was looking for someone to understand that there should be checks and balances for all employees.

I know that it can be difficult addressing matters with schools as a part-time employee. You might feel that you do not have a leg to stand on, but you do. If you are a good instructor (and I am) with great evaluations, then ultimately it will be the school's loss if administrators cannot address your concerns or at least acknowledge your work. The school I spoke about earlier now has incentives for adjunct faculty, such as monetary bonuses for adjunct faculty who do exceptional work. Even if you never receive a bonus, I would think the school would at least send a T-shirt or some type of acknowledgment for online instructors. If all else fails, remember that I am there with you, along with other online instructors. Hopefully, you will be as lucky as I am and not have many, if any, administrator disasters and work for great schools. If you do have administrator disasters, remember that you are not alone.

ANOTHER STORM BREWING

And just as I was writing this chapter, I felt another storm brewing. I received an evaluation for one of my online classes. The school administrators were changing department heads continuously, and just my luck, mine resulted in being placed with a senile supervisor. I am sorry, that was a bit harsh. He really turned out to be a nice guy, but I was thinking at the time when I read my evaluation, *Who Let this Disaster in My Classroom?*

The way this situation started was when the school sent an e-mail saying that students did not have to answer discussion questions for the Easter holiday but had to complete the other assignments. Naturally, I did not respond to the discussions boards because there were only a few students who participated that week. If the school offers a break, students take it, and that is great for an instructor. My new department head decided to do a review of my class that week. He said that I needed a stronger presence in my class and my interaction was unsettling in the discussion forum. I wanted to mentally blow the roof off the building—if that were possible. I know that this was an honest mistake, but I called him to clarify that this was Easter week and that the school had sent an e-mail about not responding in the discussion forums. My supervisor commented that other instructors had responded. I explained to him that there were only a couple of students who made replies because they had followed the memo—which was apparently ambiguous. In speaking with him, I still did not feel comfortable after I hung up the telephone. Somewhere I felt a poor review was on my record.

You know by now that I love teaching online and I do my best, so to receive a poor review in error really upset me. In fact, I was beyond upset, and I had a headache trying to stifle curse words. So, I wrote about it. Not only did I write about it in this book, but I also sent an e-mail to my supervisor as well as to his boss. I wanted to be sure that the information was documented in writing on my part, and I needed an outlet to vent. But it still annoyed the heck out of me. It was another situation where I felt alone, where I felt that somewhere someone was thinking that I was a slacker. What really made me angry is that I had to request that he review another week, such as prior to the holiday or an upcoming week, to really assess my student interaction. Why hadn't he had enough sense to say that he would do this before I initiated the request? It goes to show, no matter what you do, sometimes your best efforts are not acknowledged in your classroom.

Unfortunately, situations and misunderstandings like these occur in our careers and lives. After I sent my e-mails, the school administrators apologized for the oversight. Yeah, yeah, yeah. What else can I say? That is the gist of my administrator disasters. Don't mess with me! You are not the boss of me! I am still trying to be the master of my online class domain, and I type that with a smile. On a more serious note, my department head and I eventually mended our differences.

14

Assessments Hanging on the Edge

IT IS A SCARY situation when something or someone is hanging on the edge; the outcome is uncertain. If you were to ask me my opinion of online assessments, my answer would be that I think tests online are scarcely hanging on to the edge in distance education. Assessments evaluate knowledge that students have obtained in the classroom. In a traditional classroom, students are tested on a subject without the book, unless it is an open-book test, and instructors can assess what students have retained without any uncertainties. Online tests have to be designed so that even if a student does use his or her textbook as a source, an instructor can assess knowledge obtained. How does one do this?

I noticed that in my English courses, students had to take grammar quizzes from Web sites the school had contracted with. This is a good tool to build directly into a course that can assess student learning and that is automatically scored. Unfortunately, sometimes when schools use outside Web sites, there are technical issues that cannot be resolved unless students contact the vendor's technical support. This can be time-consuming and confusing for the student. The quizzes are good assessments, but it would be ideal to place tests directly into the school's distance-education software.

Online assessments need a facelift. A more innovative way of assessing students' retention is necessary in order for online schools to continually appeal to the masses and be competitive.

Here are some suggestions for unique assessments:

- Final exams moderated by the instructor

- Assessments that require students to research businesses online and report their findings

- Assessments that combine all types of tests, such as short answer, multiple choice, true and false, and matching, into one

- Assessments that require students to become the expert on the subject and interview professionals in their fields of interest

The main innovative type of assessment that should be added to online classes is a testing system built directly into the software, like the quizzes I discussed with regard to my English courses. This type of testing system should be able to handle final exams that are structured just as midterms and final exams are in a traditional setting. Here again, this may take some creative programming skills.

I truly support distance education being set up differently than a traditional school because that is what makes online learning unique. However, I think more credibility is needed with the tests. It's almost as if the message needs to be pervasive that online learning is unique, yet requires work. Newly designed tests should be the trailer to attract online participants. I sense a strong disconnect and misconception that online learning is a way to receive an easy degree; that is far from the truth. I guess I want to see less questioning of the validity of online learning. The assessments can involve simulations where the student has to go through a process and select the correct answer without feedback. The preparation for the exam can provide feedback, but final exams need to illustrate an overall retention of coursework. As indicated in this book, online learning should be the trailblazer for unique testing and instructional lessons. Assessments need a facelift, as do the tracking devices to see how far students have come from the start of class throughout their duration in college. There have to be more original types of testing than true or false and multiple choice questions for online students. I am not a programmer, but maybe I will write a script for online testing!

WHAT IS A RUBRIC?

Having a rubric for assignments may help bridge the gap and reduce student/instructor conflict. A rubric is a tool that lists the scores and criteria for assignments. Having a standard rubric is ideal, but as assignments and requirements change, so must the rubric. Rubrics should include enough detail yet be simple enough so that students can understand and comprehend the grading standards.

You will notice that most rubrics are prewritten with general text. It might help if you add specific criteria for your subject and take the time to include additional comments on students' written assignments and/or the assignment in general. The rubric is another opportunity to teach. Review the comments that I placed in the sample rubric.

Sample Rubric Written Assignments

Student selected appropriate topic for assignment, included a thesis and supporting facts.	25
The content exemplifies college writing. Comment: Here discuss problems or comment about students' writing. You can comment on whether the student met the qualifications for the assignment. You will want to address grammar concerns or sentence structure errors. If your school has a writing lab, you may want to suggest additional help for the student.	50
Paper is written in APA, MLA, or simple citations style Comment: Here discuss problems and comment on student citation and formatting.	25

Total Percentage: ____ out of 100 percent
Total Points: ____ out of 25 points
Student Score: _____

Example

Shirley's Scores

Student selected appropriate topic for assignment, included a thesis and supporting facts. Comments: Hi, Shirley. Your topic, "How do bad habits affect bad health?" is a great topic for an expository essay. As the reader, my curiosity was piqued immediately as to the possible viewpoints that you would discuss in this essay. Your thesis was clear and set the tone for your essay.	20

The content exemplifies collegiate writing. Comments: Overall, the content was good and you met the requirements for the assignment. There are a few areas that you need to work on with regard to your grammar. First, in formal essays, try to avoid using contractions. Simply write out the entire word. Also, when writing an expository essay, write from third-person point of view. Most essays are written in third-person point of view (he, she, it, or they) unless it is your opinion. Then it would be written in first-person point of view. Always avoid second-person point of view, "you," in formal essays. For more information on grammar rules, please review my lecture for week two and visit the school's writing lab.	35
Paper is written in APA, MLA, or simple citations style Comments: Overall, your citations are great. You only need to remember that your header (shorter version of your title) should be embedded in your document with page numbers. Please see the sample document in class on how to format this correctly.	20

Total Percentage Possible: 100 percent
Total Possible Points: 25 points
Student Points: 75 x 25 percent
Final Score: 18.75

You can add criteria that are pertinent to each assignment. Rubrics that do not have detailed criteria can leave room for student grade conflict. Then you will receive disaster e-mails from students inquiring why their grades are low. Also, I noticed that some students do not review rubrics. Some students do not know what a rubric is exactly. You may want to let students know that this is the grading criteria for a particular assignment. Please be sure that rubrics are posted in an area by the written assignments and place an announcement to let students know that the rubric is available before the assignment due date.

Other criteria that you might consider and edit as part of your rubric are as follows:

- Content
  - » Content is organized and comprehensive
  - » Sentences clearly identify the writer's purpose
  - » Writer selected appropriate word choice for assignment
  - » The thesis is well-developed
  - » Research supports thesis statement and is consistent throughout the assignment

- Grammar
  - » Punctuation is clear and consistent throughout submission
  - » Document is spell checked
- Organization and Structure
  - » Paragraph spacing is correct, as well as the setup of the submission
  - » Title page is formatted correctly
  - » Citations are correct and used appropriately

These are positive statements that can be turned into poor or not met statements in your rubric if the student did not meet the requirements. Again, you can add a comment section to explain areas of improvement. When in doubt about how to design an effective rubric, go back to the basics and set up a chart like the one below with pertinent criteria to your course.

	GOOD	AVERAGE	POOR
Content Comments	Content is clear and without errors. Sentences flow easily with transitional words throughout the essay. The thesis is well-developed	Content has few errors. Sentences are clear in some parts of the essay. The thesis is stated but needs more development.	Content is incomplete. Sentences are not clear throughout the document. There is no clear thesis.
Grammar Comments	GOOD Essay contains no grammar and spelling errors.	AVERAGE Essay contains few grammar and spelling errors.	POOR Essay contains many grammar and spelling errors.
Organization Comments	GOOD Citations and references are used and formatted correctly. Title page is formatted correctly. Paragraphs are clear and formatted correctly.	AVERAGE Citations and references were used, but there are some citation errors. Title page has few errors. Paragraphs have few structuring errors.	POOR Citations and references are not used in this essay. The title page is not formatted correctly. Paragraphs are not structured correctly.

You can always type more information or place a comment in the comments field if you want to say something specific to the student regarding his or her submission. I attended an online instructors' meeting, and in the Q&A session, an instructor asked, "How do I know if I'm being too critical with students' grades?" I don't believe the administrators expected her to ask this question. I say this because she addressed the question in general, and they answered the question by using an example about citations, saying that instructors should not strictly critique students who are not citing sources properly. This instructor was in need of a support system and resources. She needed a place where she could compare and discuss grading procedures. Honestly, there is no way to answer this because since its inception, grading has been subjective. In my opinion, having a rubric for each assignment will make grading less subjective. Instructors can always refer the student back to the criteria in the rubric when in doubt. Rubrics can be tweaked for any assignment. They can be used as a guide to help with parameters in student grading.

When the instructor asked the question wondering if her grading was "too critical," it provided more insight on my observations in this book. Online instructors do not have all the answers. We are learning teaching techniques as we go in hopes that we are being effective online instructors. There is a need for a central location for online instructors to share best practices. I see that the need is so great. Instructors seem to want to know that someone understands or possibly has a more efficient way of completing a teaching task.

Another good idea is to have discussion question rubrics. This may help reduce some discussion board forum disasters as well. This can be added to your syllabus or placed in the discussion forum. Here is an example of a discussion question rubric.

Discussion Question Rubric

Points	Description
4–5	Discussion response added value to the class. Response specifically included information from the required reading material, included personal experiences, and introduced new ideas to the class. Student met the requirements for the discussion question.
2–3	Discussion response included valuable information but did not relate to the topic as required. Student met the minimum requirements for the discussion question.
0–1	Discussion response did not target the topic of the week or introduce any new ideas, personal experiences, or textbook material to the class. Student did not meet the minimum requirements for the discussion question.

You could inform students that points will be reduced for grammar errors in your discussion question rubrics, or you can announce this in class and keep your rubrics simple.

15

Americans with Disability Act

HAVING A CLASS THAT adheres to the Americans with Disability Act is necessary for online learning. You will not know if your students are disabled unless they inform you. These students might have to initiate being classified as disabled in order to take advantage of the school's services, in my experience. Some schools do not allow instructors to suggest that students contact disability services if they notice students are struggling. I have had students inform me they were disabled and needed extra time submitting their work. Significant amounts of time are usually not needed because disabled students can actually do the work. It is more important to be cognizant that it is possible to have students who have poor eyesight or poor hearing and who need versatile instructional material to meet their needs. Instructional designers create courses with this in mind by using large print, audio textbooks using mp3 files, and visuals for anyone struggling in this area. Each school should have a center to assists online disabled students. Students usually will initiate when they need these services.

I have experienced one significant student who I did want to recommend to disability services or any service the school had available to assist her. I spoke with her advisor because her responses were becoming disruptive to students. This young lady, whom I will call Alegra, appeared to have mental issues. She was the sweetest and most endearing student I have ever met online, but her assignments were always off topic. For example, the assignment might be to write about reading strategies, and Alegra would submit work about evolution. She was so smart; I didn't know what she was talking about half the time. When I called her to do outreach and tried to help her in class, she told me that she was glad that I called and that Jesus Christ died for our sins. I was happy to hear this—but this did not have anything to do with the class. This was her pattern. She tried to help everyone "get saved" in class, and it annoyed some students. She also had the tendency to send chain e-mails to students and me with smiley faces, winks, and other emoticons that I still cannot create and do not have an interest to create on a computer keyboard. Alegra failed the course because she only submitted partial work. When she submitted partial work, it was always about anything other than the assignment. I was saddened by her failing the course because I truly did want to help this student. The school was aware of her situation, and she was offered disability services and declined.

As an online instructor, you can only do your best and beyond and accept what you cannot change. It is a good idea to be aware of the school's services for students in need. Alegra had to re-take the course.

16

No More Disasters

I WISH I COULD say that this is true. There will be no more student disasters someday, but as long as there is e-mail, distance education, students, instructors, faculty, and prewritten courses, there will be student disasters. There will always be students who send their work at the last minute, or should I reiterate, the last couple of days of class; students who are upset because they believe you judged them unfairly; students trying to teach the class better than you; students trying to intimidate you; students personifying a renegade spirit; and students who challenge you every step of the way. You can say it is raining in your hometown, and they will say, "I have to disagree with you," even when they live in another region. I have only been teaching online for close to two years. I am sure as time progresses I will have a new perspective about online disasters. I am still encouraged, though, because I know that with each disaster growth is inevitable. Sometimes it is not instantaneous growth, but it is priceless growth.

PERSONAL DISASTERS

The Roof Caved in on My House

It never occurred to me that I would have a personal disaster as I was writing this book. I was in between classes and had some downtime. I only had two courses, which I could easily manage. I was moving into a new house, so I asked my mother and sister to come for a visit. The weekend before their arrival, my mother had a stroke. My mother, the catalyst in my life, had fallen ill—my mother, the one who chose my major in college, my best friend. She hadn't even been sick. She just hadn't been to a doctor in decades, nor could I persuade her to go for an annual visit. I was persistent about regular checkups, and she was persistent about not listening to me. The roof had caved in on my house. This was too close to home. I quickly packed my laptop and two pairs of jeans and told my husband, "Let's go." My mother lives in a different state. I arrived five hours later to find that she was stable. Her left side was immobilized, with minor damage to the brain. God was there; I could feel him. I did not log in that day. I waited until early the next morning to check with my students. I spent the night at the hospital, so I was able to log on when I calmed down.

I started to think, *What happens to online instructors when personal disasters occur, such as a sick loved one, the death of a loved one, children going astray, spouses acting like donkeys, etc.? How does one stay focused?* Luckily, I did not have any student disasters during my stay in my hometown. When I returned home, I found that I was more stressed. My mother was in rehabilitation services by then and recovering fast. Thank God. I still could not stay for an extended visit because I had to take care of my move. I found that I was impersonal with some students and supplied curt responses. One student e-mailed me and said, "I am sorry to bother you." This was after I sent her an e-mail because she was sending me assignments instead of placing them in the assigned area in class. My tone must have been rude in my e-mail. I really couldn't recall, but this snapped me back into reality. It was something about the "bother you" that made me realize that I cannot lose my professionalism in my grief. I guess if it ever gets unbearable for you in the personal disasters, you can always ask someone to step in for you by contacting your administrators. I am not sure if there is a policy in case of emergencies for online instructors. If not, there should be one or some type of instructor buddy system. If you can manage to grade papers, respond to students, and complete your daily tasks in the midst of your personal disaster, that would be a great feat. Luckily, I was able to complete my courses and all my responsibilities.

As my mother started to recover, I noticed that she was aloof. I was not used to her behaving in this manner, considering that we usually talked twenty times a day. I know that it was a result of the stroke. She always calls me "Martha—Martha" from the Bible. Martha was the young lady who was busy making Jesus comfortable and making sure the house was in order while her sister, Mary, was sitting down listening to Jesus speak. She said I had the spirit of Martha, a worrier. I guess she was aloof because she did not want to worry me about her health—as if that were possible.

It was when I realized this that I became more sympathetic to my students' needs. Sometimes it is easy to become jaded when you hear countless stories or excuses from students. I had a student at the time whose husband was sick. She needed extra time to submit her assignments. I sent her an e-mail explaining that I understood and that it had not been a great week for me as well. We e-mailed a little about how having to take care of responsibilities when family members are sick can be taxing. It was then that I realized that I need love from my students occasionally. The instructor had become the student. The instructor had become a person with "raw" emotions. I do care for my students, that is a given, but this experience made me more cognizant that at times students truly do have unforeseen issues. I had a new perspective than when I wrote my "Excuses—You've Been Served" chapter. Yes, students have to submit their work, but I need to be more receptive and make sure that I am not jaded. It was then that I became more consistent with sending out my "checking in" e-mails.

E-mail

Hi, students,

I am checking with you to see how class is going. Have you checked your grades up until this point? Do you have any questions/problems? Please keep me posted and let me know how I can assist. I am here to help.

Have a great weekend.

Professor Smith

Another point I want to make that I observed in my personal disaster was with regard to my mother's doctor. The physician in the intensive care unit was strange. I know some doctors have a tendency to come in the patient's room quickly and leave before family members have a chance to drill them, but this physician was extremely fast. He would review the chart at the door and ask my mother how she was feeling without waiting for an answer and then leave the rest for the nurses to attend. I guess that was his routine. I couldn't believe he was actually getting paid to do what appeared to be nothing. The medical profession needs a facelift as well. Luckily, my mother had other great doctors and therapists. But this experience made me think about my outreach efforts to students. One of my colleges requires instructors to do outreach for inactive students. It can be time-consuming calling and recording notes about the outreach. Some days I just do not want to do it. However, I am always mindful of the "what ifs." On one particular day, I was mindful of the "what ifs" with regard to my mother. What if someone taking care of my mother was lax? What if a physician did not take care of his patients because he was tired, his rounds were almost complete, and he could not revisit a patient's chart and notice medicine conflicts? These are our jobs. It is unacceptable to be sloppy. I think that is why I push so hard to follow up with students. It's my job. It's my calling. If everyone were lax in their jobs, the world would be in more trouble than our current economic state.

Out of all disasters, the ultimate disaster would be the one that you did not grow from as an instructor or one that did not provide a life lesson. The disaster that does not cause you to re-examine your effectiveness, stance, disposition, and feelings regarding online learning and your students is truly a disaster.

17

Sunshine

HAVE YOU EVER SEEN the sunset or a sunrise? It is a powerful sight. The color scheme alone is beautiful and vibrant. Most of the time, online learning is as beautiful as a sunrise. On average, I have more than two hundred students every term, and only three might be difficult per term or every other term. That is pretty great! The disasters that I wrote about were all isolated events. Online teaching is very rewarding, and the good has outweighed the disasters. The examples of overcoming some of these challenges are practical, and you might have used them already in your classes. In the disasters, you must take a break before you say something to a student that you will eventually be sorry for and that you truly did not mean. The beauty of online learning is that it is mostly asynchronous. You can respond usually anytime within twenty-four hours. So, take your much-needed breaks and try your best to see beyond the headaches and embrace the sunshine.

REMNANTS

The following information explains a few more details that you might find beneficial from my online teaching experiences in your classes. I learned that critical thinking is a factor in e-learning. You have to be able to exercise it, sometimes immediately, as an online instructor. But if you are like me, sometimes it is a judgment call and you really are not sure how the situation will play out. I encountered a student who missed the first couple of weeks of school and wanted to make up his work. I explained that he would have to complete a significant amount of work and that assignments accomplished in haste could affect his grade. I asked him to contact his advisor for other options, meaning that he could withdraw from the class instead of risk a failing grade. He explained that he had contacted his advisor and that she told him to contact me. I did not know if he had or had not spoken with his advisor—but I explained what the risks were, and I had to exercise critical thinking. I did not allow the student to make up discussion responses because I like for those to be active, but I did allow the written assignments to be completed. At one point, I wanted to tell the student that it was impossible, especially with the grade risk—but he appeared to be sincere and was persistent. After I analyzed the situation, I accepted his proposal and provided a due date that he had to meet. He was able to complete some of his missed work and pass the class with a decent grade.

Another time I had office hours on instant messaging and a student came to my office. Here's the crux of the situation:

Marissa sent me an instant message saying that she was disabled and that she did not leave the house. Therefore, it was going to be difficult for her to find someone to interview for her final project. I asked her about her area of interest, and she said that it was Web design. I told her to search the Internet and call someone and ask for a few moments of his or her time for an interview. I started to provide her with my Web designer's contact information, but then I would have been doing the assignment for her. I started to provide this information because I was not thinking critically, I was thinking emotionally. I wanted to help my disabled student. If I had naturally thought critically before my hesitation, then I would have known that this student could pick up the telephone and speak with someone and did not necessarily have to leave the house. She did inform me that she was able to use her arms. I did not provide her with my Web designer's name because Web designers are easy to find and speak with simply by searching the Internet for a contact.

It is important to exercise judgment and try to think critically by evaluating the situation before making suggestions and answering questions. Even if you have to recant your suggestion, at least you would have thought logically and avoided potential disasters.

SETTING THE ATMOSPHERE

I do believe that your atmosphere has a lot to do with your mood. As online instructors, we can travel with our laptops to great places to set the atmosphere. Some of our cities have mountains that are nearby, great parks, and even awesome cafes. We can embrace nature, spruce up our home offices to reflect our styles, or go to an area in our homes that is just for us to interact with our students. Set your atmosphere. Make it great! Make it a place for you where you can think before interacting with your students. Make it a place where quiet can rest on your shoulders when having to type many e-mails.

Also, set your cognitive atmosphere by cultivating your teaching methods. Some schools offer professional development opportunities for online faculty to enroll. These are great learning experiences that you can take online for less than an hour. If you do not find any of interest, look online for one- or two-day workshops in your city. Are you interested in learning how to resolve conflict online? Are you interested in learning a new graphics program? Do an inventory of your interests. You can always be a lifelong learner. Set your atmosphere in whatever form you choose. You will be empowered with knowledge. That is not a recipe for a disaster.

18

I Survived the Disaster

I THINK I MAY have found the title for my next book! *I Survived the Disaster.* As I was preparing to write the close to this book, I wondered what I could say to help you in the challenging and perhaps lonely times as an online instructor. How could I help make being an online instructor feel natural yet tolerable for you in the event that you feel no one else understands? In my search for an answer for you, I realized that I am moving gently—yet sometimes roughly—forward in my experiences as an online instructor in this great professional career that God has blessed and trusted me with completing. I am taking you (my fellow online instructors) with me as we glide through rough, innovative, and unfamiliar terrain. To have all great days in school in this life would be fantasy, but this—this is reality. And if all else fails, re-read my book and laugh at some of my disasters, and then you will know you are not alone.

Reflections

School Days

One of the hardest disciplines in life is learning patience. A student once asked me if it would be considered plagiarism if she were to purchase a prewritten essay for ten dollars off the Internet and cite the Web site where she bought the essay. I wanted to respond, "Are you kidding me?"